On graphics: tips for editors

A miscellany of practical fundamentals   Jan V. White

Lawrence Ragan Communications, Inc.   Chicago

About the author:
Jan White, author of *Editing by Design, Designing
...for Magazines, Graphic Idea Notebook,*
and *18 Ready-to-Use Grids,* is a columnist for
The Ragan Report. He is a consultant art director
who has designed or redesigned more than
100 publications in the U.S. and South America.
He also teaches seminars on graphic presentation
for Folio, Lawrence Ragan Communications, Inc.,
and other organizations, including New York
University.

Copyright 1981
by Jan V. White
ISBN 0-931368-06-5

Published by
Lawrence Ragan Communications, Inc.
407 South Dearborn Street
Chicago, IL 60605

Making the most of newsletters	**4**
Getting attention	**6**
Using typewriters to best advantage	**8**
Getting typewriter type to look right	**16**
Where to get free art	**20**
Magic and sleight of hand	**22**
Why use rules?	**23**
Grids	**24**
Achieving legibility	**28**
Boxes: what's in them for you?	**30**
Breaking up the text	**32**
Mugshots—yecch!	**40**
If the pocket is right, it's wrong	**46**
Left-to-right and the sticky edge	**48**
Getting an artist to draw the drawing you want	**50**
For goodness' sake, get on with it!	**54**

Making the most of newsletters

If you are doing a typewritten newsletter, do NOT introduce typeset type. A typewritten newsletter's magic is that illusory quality of a "personal" communication...the inside poop...that latest scuttlebutt. This illusion is destroyed by introduction of formal typesetting (for heads and whatnot). The typewriter then becomes a gimmick that the recipient sees through right away; and it bothers him, since typewriter type isn't the most legible of faces—so why, he wonders, are they making me plough through this stuff when it is obviously phony?

By all means use typeset type for the masthead and other such background information; but do it in such a way that it is obviously separated from the text and connotes a pre-printed form like a letterhead, into which the body of the text has been inserted. Second color is ideal as tip-off here.

A newsletter is not a magazine

Avoid making the newsletter look like a magazine: it cannot help but look puny by comparison. Instead, build on the positive attributes of a newsletter: the intimate, personal contact between sender and recipient. To achieve this personal touch, eschew magazine-y techniques: don't use slick stock; don't use regular columns; don't think in terms of articles with formal headlines and decks and subheads; don't attempt to dress things up to "catch the reader" (he or she is already caught—at least, that is the assumption you work on).

Instead, limit yourself to the absolute minimum of graphic means to get your thoughts across; the rationale: you haven't the time to fancy things up. Use paper that is anything but white and coated; the rationale: make it look as much like a letter as possible, and most letterheads use colored stock nowadays. Use short and concise items instead of long essays; and in scale with the smallness of the items, replace formal headlines with boldface lead-ins, underscored wording, first lines that poke out into the left-hand margin and thus catch the eye ...or other nonmagazine techniques.

Experiment with color

Add colorfulness to the product. Color creates mood, helps personality, is likely to be cheerful, and should certainly make your product look different from other people's. Colored stock is available at very little more than ordinary white stock and most paper houses have a dozen or more pale colors to choose from. Most of them are, admittedly, pastel-pale and wishy-washy, so you must choose with discrimination and courage (avoid pink and powder blue—and telegram-yellow!). But pick out a color that is likely to be available for a long time; there is constant change in this business and if a hue isn't selling well enough, the manufacturer will withdraw it and peddle a different one.

However, just a colored stock by itself may not be enough of a difference between you and everyone else. Just printing in black ink on a tan paper isn't enough. You have to use colored ink as well. That way your individuality will sing out much more visibly. What color? The sky's the limit. The printer might help with samples and suggestions; but a small investment in a test run using three or four different colors *on your stock* is well worth it in the long run, because, once you have found the combination that works for you, it will be with you for years. Because it will give you individuality and recognition at first glance, whatever you do (however uninspired it might be in black-on-white) will appear that much more interesting.

Choose a stock for its character

The texture and "snap" of a paper are essential ingredients in the "feel" of a printed piece. Your words printed on a material that has a definite character of its own can gain much impact and believability and dignity from it. (On the other hand, to carry weight and importance, they have to be very powerful indeed, if they are run off in standard black ink on good old nondescript white, floppy, shiny paper.) Just increasing the weight—i.e. thickness—of your stock doesn't make that much difference. All that does is raise your postage rates. You have to go beyond plain weight, to consider things like: smoothness/roughness; floppiness/stiffness; smoothness/crinkliness; thinness/fatness; and, most of all, the sound it makes when handled. Check what the paper merchant (or printer) might suggest for you. And remember that the cost of the stock is probably no more than five percent of the total cost of producing the piece—if that! So even if you increase your paper cost by half as much again, you are still only dealing in peanuts.

The logo is you

Personalize the newsletter with a distinctive logotype (masthead, name). Make it sing your individuality. It is your trademark, so don't be satisfied with just having it set in plain type (however peculiar that typeface you choose may be), but be sure to make it somehow personalized. It is worth the extra investment, because you become YOU—not just anybody. How is this done? By a designer, who plays with the raw material of the type, combines it, slurs it, runs characters together, overlaps them, superimposes them, ties them together with lines or extensions or whatnot...and, in effect, comes up with a monogrammed version of the name itself.

The feeling of the new logo will have a great effect on the atmosphere and character of the newsletter: old-fashioned but serious; playful but exciting; up-to-the minute but aware of the Eternal Verities; conservative but with-it enough to be with-it...that sort of thing.

Once you have achieved the appropriate graphic embodiment of your image in the logo, avoid cluttering it up and thus reducing its impact and visibility. Keep the graphic static away from it: have it sit in a bath of white space—clear, uncluttered, crisply demarcated. Keep the volume number, date and explanatory blurb away from the logo itself so the name can be seen alone. That stuff should be concentrated in a small area of its own. Thus you achieve three distinct elements on your front page: the name, blurb stuff, and the first story.

The story will probably be good and achieve impact. If your logo is good, your story will appear twice as good, because they'll realize that they are reading that good story in YOUR newsletter. They'll remember that. And the spinoff is future recognition, familiarity, acceptance and readers' loyalty. What else can one ask for?

Getting attention

This is supposed to be a design-oriented book. So it is. But "design" is just the means to an end—that of communication. The *what* of communication is editing. The three examples shown on these pages are shown and annotated in an attempt to persuade you that *editing* must precede *designing* and that when it does, the design process becomes merely a *technique* of *editing* with no magic or "art" about it.

The examples illustrate a theory of visual editing (based on editorial thinking):

1) That which is important deserves to be made visible.

2) To make it visible, it should be bold and black (to get maximum contrast with its background); and

3) To make it visible, it should be big (because bigness equals importance).

4) It must appear in surroundings in which it is allowed to be seen without visual static all around.

The practice:

1) Look at the product—see—notice—perceive.

2) Analyze and edit (i.e. decide on that which is crucial and that which is secondary).

3) Express that analysis by making the crucial elements enormous and black, and the secondary elements tiny and pale.

4) Have the courage to chop away the surroundings that choke off the air.

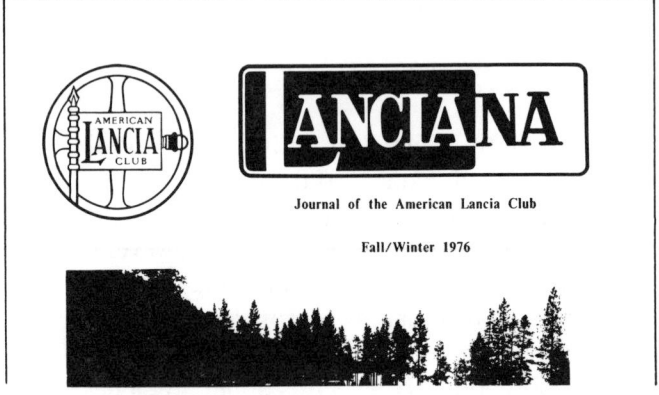

BEFORE: Nothing is dominant. Everything floats around without any evident reason. Everything appears about the same size—so it all fights. No wide empty spaces; repetition of facts (e.g. the fact that this is the journal of the Lancia Club, let alone repetition of the name itself 3 times).

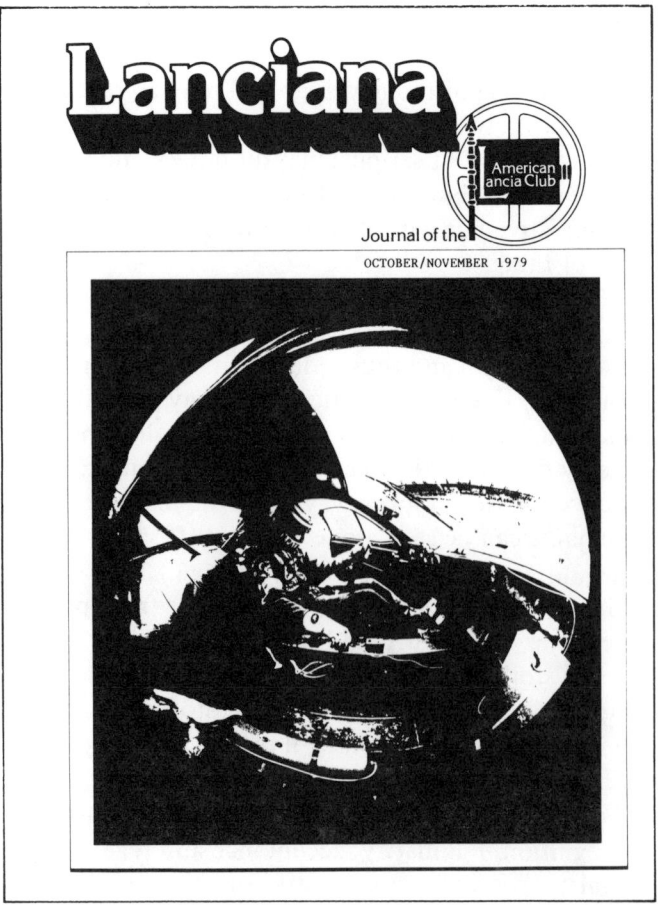

AFTER: The one thing that needs to be seen first is the logo—so it is placed at left (we read left-to-right). The letters are enlarged and strengthened with a heavy shadow. Coat of arms strengthed, yet reduced in importance by secondary placement "behind" logo. Duplications edited out. Picture anchored in position within box. Same box runs every issue with cover subject varying in size, shape etc.—yet format ensures continuation of effect and "fullness" of image by means of that frame.

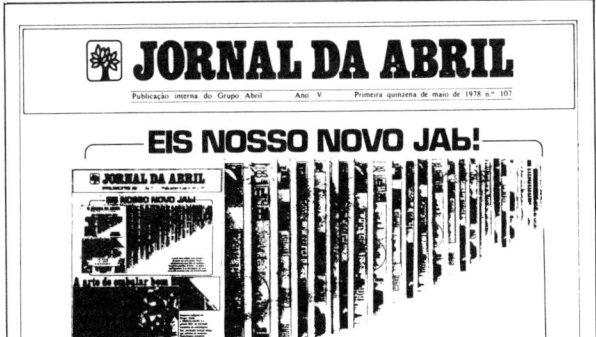

BEFORE: Good, black, large logo spoiled by surrounding it with gray stuff (including the line of minor facts placed between two rules), all put in pale box which, itself, sits in a big box. Trademark of tree arbitrarily in front of logo, whereas it refers to the name of the company, which is logically part of the small type, not the logo.

AFTER: The one important element—the logo—pops out, yet no change made in its design. The small stuff is pulled to right, combined with trademark, played down. The box-in-a-box is replaced with a simple light rule across the top to identify the edge of the space, and a bold one across the bottom to identify top of editorial space beneath the logo. Simpler, lighter, and more colorful.

BEFORE: Typical newspaper flag. Name is camouflaged by ancillary matter displayed illegibly beneath it in four different typefaces, centered on the space with no relationship to the oval diagram of the round table.

AFTER, Step 2: Enlarging newspaper to full size. Redesigning logo in more contemporary (though conservative) face; placing it within unsullied, dramatic white area defined by vertical rule at left and horizontal rule across top. Right-hand edge of "box" is left open, though it is defined by the flush-right edge of the ancillary information set in tiny type and suspended from the end of the rule across the top, at right. Bold rule adds "color" and splits editorial matter from flag. This scheme not only works well, but has found acceptance from subscribers, advertisers and prizes from competitions. So simple! But it needed guts to do it—both publishing, editing and design courage.

AFTER, Step 1: Same space used as before but defined by added horizontal rules. Ancillary information is tied into the oval by centering and tightening it and setting it all same size, all-caps. "Millbrook" and "Round Table," seen against a clear, dramatic foil of white space, can be read from across the street.

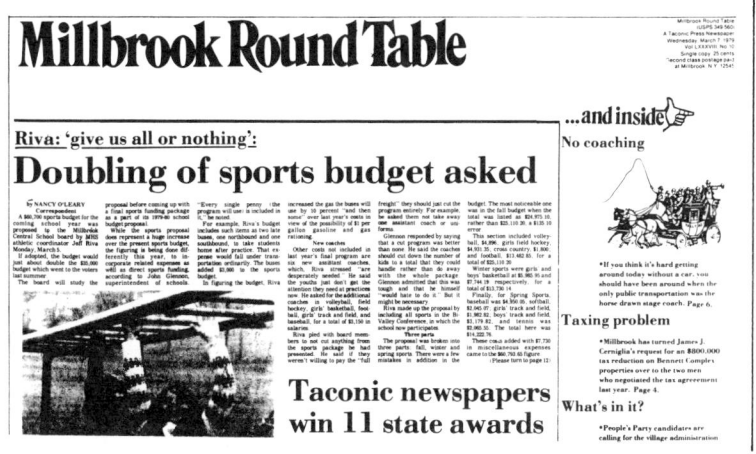

7

Using typewriters to best advantage

In printed pieces that use typewriter type throughout, the major problem is how to signal story-starts. Two major areas need exploring: how to separate stories and how to make the headlines pop out.

1

Spaces

Do not separate paragraphs within a story by a full line of space. Instead, have a deep indent to signal the start of a fresh paragraph. That way you reserve spacing for separating stories from each other, without wasting precious space. Were you to allow a line of space between paragraphs, you would have to leave at least two or even three to separate stories in order to make the difference obvious enough at first glance. The actual result of this is to make your overall texture thin, too much white space. And that is not good PR in a newsletter: it may well make the recipient feel that there isn't enough value for the money.

So: tighten, where it makes sense to do so. If you are afraid of too much massiveness of type without that line of space between the paragraphs, deepen the indent, up to half a line length. That fjord of lightness flowing into the gray cliffs will pull the eye in and will do the break-up trick for you.

Headlines

You need "color" to make them visible. More ink coverage, greater concentration, thicker texture, and—most important of all—a clearly demarcated area of space within which the headline is to be viewed. This white space need not be large or wasteful. It does need to be clearly, geometrically demarcated so that it appears obviously deliberate and planned to be that way. The secret here is simple: if there are two handled the same way, that implies they are deliberately planned that way. That's one of the wonderful things about repetition. Another is that you don't have to reinvent the wheel every time. . .but back to headlines:

Example A: Break every headline into two lines: type them in all-capitals, flush left, with no extra space between the lines. Break the lines by sense-making phrasing. You already have maximum ink coverage from the characters themselves, but now you add underscoring under each line, plus *above* the top line—so your head becomes a triple-decker sandwich. Go beyond the obvious, though: run those underscores out further at the right to a total sense-making width of 24 characters, let's say.

Then start your text a couple of characters further over to the right, indenting the first four lines of text cleanly that way. This will leave two lines of white space beneath the headline, when the fifth text line starts flush left with the headline (which sounds complicated to describe. . .look at Example A: it's easy). If you use a pattern for all your heads, you automatically create a totally "different" feel to your piece, yet it is child's play to produce on the typewriter.

```
THIS IS A HEADLINE           Here starts the text of this article and it is
TYPED IN ALL-CAPITALS        indented the same number of characters from the
                             left for a total of four lines of type; this trick
                             allows the space within which the headline is
placed to be clearly visible and pop out from the surrounding text matter.
Here is another line of dummy type to illustrate this simple idea. Another minor
variation might be the following illustration. Allow 2 lines of space, then...


THIS IS ANOTHER HEADLINE     Here starts the text of the next article, below
TYPED IN TWO LINES           the overscore that extends all the way across the
                             page, thus separating stories from each other most
                             obviously and effectively. The problem with typing
this sort of thing is that it is not good form to have typos visible... that makes
life very difficult if you are a lousy typist like the author of this article...




          THE NUMBER OF OPTIONS FOR DESIGNING with a
               typewriter is very limited. It becomes
               an exercise in ingenuity and mathematics.
               How much to indent, where, and with what.
               Hanging the heads out into the space
               at left is a most effective means of
               letting our attention focus onto the
               starts of things. But we must add as
               much color (i.e. blackness) to those
               points as possible. Hence the additional
               underscoring and overscoring.
          HERE IS ANOTHER SUCH HEADLINE  which inter-
               rupts the flow of the text very ef-
               fectively. But it is not very strong
               in signalling something NEW. A line
               of space preceding it would add to
               its headline quality:

          THIS STARTS SOMETHING DIFFERENT: and a colon
               helps the idea of the start along...
               see how that line of extra space makes
               the headline look that much more im-
               portant?
```

Example B: Type your text to a narrow column (55 elite characters or so). Impose the text on the page in such a way as to allow the maximum amount of space along the left-hand edge (make the left margin as fat as possible). That will be the space in which you insert your headlines. However, to avoid wasting space between stories, allow only two lines of skipped space. The last line of your headline will be stacked up above it, flush left, hopefully five or six high, so it is worth looking at. Type them in all-caps, underscore them, or do anything else that makes sense on the typewriter and is easy to repeat. Repetition is of the essence: that's what creates a "personality."

```
                        This is the end of a normal text piece, typed at a fairly
                        narrow measure. The advantage of that narrowness is that it
                        allows the left-hand margin of the page to be much wider than
THIS IS THE             is customary, and thus yields a useful space for placement
FIRST LINE              of the display headline at left.
OF A NICE LONG
HEADLINE THAT
READS INTO THE TEXT, THUS: Here starts the text of the succeeding story. Note
                        that there are two lines of space skipped between the two
                        stories. The headline can have any number of short, stacked
                        lines in the left-hand margin, so long as the last of those
                        lines reads into the first line of the text.
```

Ultimately,
there are
only a few
simple things one can do with a typewriter.
                      Beyond this, individual good
                      sense and subjective taste take
                      over. It boils down to a matter
Here you   *of mixing 'n matching of gimmicks*
thought   *and tricks to produce the best*
you were   *recipe for the project at hand.*
reading
some philosophy and it is nothing of the sort.
                      It is padding, woffling, humbug,
                      twaddle, prattle, blather, piffle,
But what   gobbledegook, gibberish, rodomon-
interesting   tade, balderdash, inanity, bushwa!
fresh
technique to tuck a lot of stuff in a page.
                      And make each unit appear self-
                      contained and separate from the
                      others below and above it. The
Then you   change in faces is a great help
can start   in separating the units.
up from
scratch again, if all you have is three
                typing elements...

Example C: Have a vertical rule running up the side of the page at left. Type your headline in all-capitals in a single line, starting one character away from your vertical rule. Underscore (and overscore) your typed line, allowing the scoring lines to touch the vertical at left...but have the underscore match the wording in length. They'll look like branches on a tree trunk or flags fluttering from a mast. If you leave a line of space below the head and a couple above the head, you achieve both visibility and breakup of the stories.

```
 |
 |
 |__THIS IS A CLEVER HEADLINE THAT IS SUSPENDED FROM THE MAST__
 |   Here is the start of the text which, hopefully, the reader will be intrigued
 |   into reading through the cleverness of the headline language. Note that the
 |   first paragraph following the headline must not be indented, in order to keep
 |   the space within which the headline is seen neat and crisp.
 |        The next paragraph can well have a good and deep indent of which this
 |   is a fairly good example. Maybe the indent could be several characters deeper
 |   still?
 |
 |
```

a somewhat elementary trick to play to gain variety on the typewritten page is illustrated here:
_____Type ten characters'-worth of underscoring lines. Then start the sentence which begins the new paragraph. Complete the entire paragraph, and when it is finished, start over.
_____Those ten lines of underscoring give an unusual effect in the texture of the column. It is not necessary to leave a line of space between paragraphs when using this trick. The ten-space indents made visible by the underscore are more than enough as signals.
_____Here we go again...

_____here is a variant on the same trick
_____used in reverse pattern. Instead of
_____poking the starts of paragraphs into
_____ the body of the surrounding text,
_____why not
Poke the headline or start OUT at the left-
_____hand margin in some fashion such as
_____this one? Each line of regular type
_____starts with six characters-worth of
_____underscore. New paragraphs do not.
This is a new paragraph starting out at
_____far left followed by the normal or
_____abnormal typing method, whichever
_____way you wish to characterize it...
The advantage of this trick is the very
_____clean left-hand edge that your type
_____columns get when placed next to
_____each other. Its disadvantage? Yes,
_____it uses lots of space. But what a
_____great way to attract Attention!

Sideheads

Sometimes called "subheads." Again, visibility is important, and we must manufacture it on the typewriter, to be consistent. Take the four- or five-letter indent as described in the listing above. Type the sidehead there and keep it short; end with a colon. Underscore the space as well as the full sidehead wording, including the colon. Follow the colon with two blank spaces and a capital letter and you're in.

```
This is an example of a sidehead. It uses the same indenting used
in the lists, underscoring the space as well as the important words
themselves:

     Sidehead words:  The first initial is placed two characters after
the colon that ends the sidehead.

     Another sidehead:  You can go on making examples ad infinitum...
```

Page imposition

Messiness and inconsistency are most noticeable at the top of the pages; that is the critical area. The bottom of the page can float—nobody looks down there. The top of the pages, though, must be neatly designed, and they must be consistent. For instance, using the underscoring technique used elsewhere in the examples: allow three lines of space down from the edge of the paper. Now type an underscore, starting flush left with the text below and have it extend to the right-hand edge of the text; this is obviously somewhere in an average position, since on a normal typewriter you have a ragged-right edge. Then type the page number directly beneath the underscore, flush left. Allow two lines of empty space beneath the page number before starting the text. This pattern can be repeated on left-or right-handed pages and will help tie your publication together like a charm.

```
_____
00

the text starts here, flush left with the overscore line, two lines of
space below the page number, symbolized here by the "00".
```

12

Lists

In typeset type, we would be able to use bullets or triangles or boldface numerals or whatnot to signal series or differentness-within-an-understood-context. On a typewriter we just have the numerals, space, and horizontal rules. The numerals are too weak to stand alone (except as "hanging indents," i.e., outside the left-hand margin). So it is necessary to build them up with gimmickry to make them pop: a good way is to type them flush left, allow three or four characters of space before the start of the text itself. But then to formalize the arrangement, underscore the numeral, the empty spaces and the first letter of the text. The underlining adds a touch of color; the clearly defined white space becomes a surprise; flush-lefting the numeral gives the idea that this is part of a running story; and it is all easy to manufacture.

```
This is an example of handling lists within the body of the text.
Although it is not too wise to allow full lines of space between items
normally, it helps the legibility of lists to do so:

1    On the seventh character start the first word of the copy; then
continue flush left in the second line. Underscore the numeral, the
empty spaces, and the first initial of the text.

2    Repeat the pattern precisely -- and you have a well-working trick
to emphasize your list makeup.
```

H. Kenneth Hansen of the Public Information Committee of the Society for Technical Communication has some additional advice. He uses two techniques for handling lists. "As the need arises," says Hansen, "use bullets (yes, your typewriter does have a bullet key) or the dash-dash system."

He identifies the "bullet key" as the lower case *o*. It's simple to use. Hansen offers these guidelines:

```
        o   Preceding each item in the list, just tap
            the lower case o on your keyboard.

        o   Depending on the column width and your tastes,
            indent or type flush left.

        o   Double space between entries.

        o   You'll find this method especially suited for
            entries with two or more lines and multi-
            sentence entries.
```

The dash-dash system works best for listing items in the middle or at the end of a paragraph. Here's how Hansen uses the dash-dash:

```
              these two lines of type represent the last two
              lines of the text that precedes the list:

              -- Use dash-dash for short, one-line items.
              -- Single space between them.
              -- Double space above and below the list.

              This represents the first line of the text that
              follows the list...
```

Hansen cautions writers/editors who use numbers (1, 2, 3...) or letters (a, b, c...) for setting off lists. "Remember," says Hansen, "numbers and letters signify something in themselves, namely a ranking of things, a succession of things, or an arrangement of things." They're great for cross-reference-by-number listings. For example, on a quiz with ten questions, each with four answers or choices (a, b, c, d), the correct answers which appear on a different page can be easily referred to.

Initials

```
       Here are some ideas on using big
       initials added to the typescript after
       the typing has been completed. They are
       simply transfer lettering rubbed on from
       sheets purchased from the art supply store
       in an incredible variety of sizes and
       styles. For an investment of around $5
       you have enough initials to do three news-
       letters (especially if you can start
       a few words with Z, Q and X!).

       T─────────────────────────────
        his is an initial cap hanging
        at left, outside the left-hand mar-
        gin, whose great advantage is that
        it adds lots of white space all
        around. Obviously at the expense
```

14

of space used for body copy. But you
can't have it both ways: if you want
drama, you've got to give something
up to achieve it. Space is the
easiest sacrifice to make.

H_____
ere you see how nicely this could
be made to work, even if you sacrifice
the dramatic indent of all the lines at left
and only indent the first line to accommodate the huge initial.

A_____
nother way to do the same sort of
        thing is this one. This is just
        about irresistible on a page.
        How can the reader NOT be be-
        guiled into reading with such
        strong visual blandishments work-
        ing on him?

N_____
obody would accuse these solutions
        of brilliance or subtlety or even
        originality. They are completely
        obvious, once you begin thinking
Yalong these lines...
_____
ou see how interesting this could
        be made to look when the particular
        trick is repeated? The white spaces
        surrounding each solution, the con-
        trast of color, the precision of the
        ruled underscore, the startling in-
        congruity of the initial itself all
        add up to character-creation with the
        simplest of means.

_____**W**_____
hat you happen to be looking
at is American Typewriter type from
sheet LG2803 of Letraset, 48pt caps.
I've used it here for two reasons:
a) I believe in using appropriate
faces wherever possible; here we use
typewriter for body copy, why not a
variant thereof for the display? and
b) I happen to have lots of it handy.
Could there be a better reason?

15

Getting typewriter type to look right

A letter written on a letterhead with an ordinary typewriter is the way we expect it to be. It is in character with our expectations and with what we consider to be in scale with the page. But a page— even of precisely the same size as the letterhead— changes its character completely, if it has a logo of a periodical instead of a plain letterhead imprinted on it. It changes our expectations. It is no longer a "letter," it has become a "publication"—even if that publication is in the form of a hybrid we call "newsletter." It is a much more formalized product that ought to LOOK different because it IS different.

Yet we are often faced with having to use the printout from our own typewriter as final copy, as "art," as "reproduction proofs." (Why? Obviously: $$, time, $$, costs, rush, $$, expense, speed, $$, budget, $$, deadlines—are there any OTHER reasons?) Then we are faced with the necessity of pretending that our typewriter has produced typeset copy. And that's a silly pretense, because it cannot succeed. There is no way that the rigidities of typewriters can be made to look like proper typeset type with all its subtleties of spacing, coloration, flexibility—developed over centuries to aid legibility. Even the most sophisticated "executive" typewriters that have characters of different widths (in which the "i" doesn't have to be as fat as an "m" as it does on ordinary typewriters) don't really come close to resembling proper type. They come closer, but I find them the worst offenders because they are neither honestly plain-old-typewriters, nor good-enough typeset type—a mugwump straddling the fence pleasing neither side. The worst offenders, of course, are the printouts produced by computers for optical scanning devices, whose wide spacing between characters disintegrates the fabric of the lettergroups by which we recognize words (i.e., read). The machines "read" letter-by-letter so for them such wide spacing is necessary. Let such travesties be reserved for *their* consumption. For us humans, let's try to stay above that in our standards. If possible....

But it may not be possible! For reasons stated above. So we must make the best of a difficult job. Anything we do may have to be a compromise between the standards we know we want, and the realities we have to work with. The simplest, most obvious adaptation of typewriter type to make it less unpalatable is to make it a bit smaller. Changing its scale immediately removes it from the nature of a letter or—Heaven forfend—the printout, into a more comfortable size appropriate to a publication. Just compare the size of type on an ordinary letter— any letter—to the type in an ordinary magazine page —TIME, for instance. The page is roughly the same size, but what a difference in scale!

Reducing the scale

The printer must turn your camera-ready copy into a printing plate. A photographic process of some sort comes into play. It is during this stage that enlargement or reduction can also be utilized. So if you submit an original that is a smidgeon larger than you want the final to be, the camera can make the adjustment for you (probably at no extra charge).

You must know two things, though: 1) how will the reduction look—how will the type "read" when it is reduced that way? and 2) how much more material can you get onto the page if you reduce the scale of the normal volume. After all, if you reduce it by, say, 10% in size, then you ought to be able to accommodate 10% more in total volume, right? Right!

To help with the first decision—how will the stuff read—here is a bunch of lines using various typing elements on my good old IBM Selectric 12-pitch. Each has been reduced to different sizes, expressed in percentages of the original. That's how printers and cameramen communicate: 100% (or focus 100.0) is same size; 90% (or focus 90.0) is ninetenths of the original size. Use this as a guide for choosing your preferred reduction. But DO experiment with your own machine first, to make sure the equivalent reduction gives the same effect. They all vary somewhat. And remember that the larger the sample, the safer will be your guess as to the final result.

What you see here are just a few snippets of lines. Anybody can buckle down and read a few lines at just about any size or degree of illegibility. But extend the bulk of those lines from a few to a full column's-worth and you have a totally different situation. What may be acceptable, if not attractive, in a small sample may well be thoroughly repulsive *en masse*. So, before committing yourself to an issue, do a dummy page and reduce it by getting a photostat to make sure it works.

P.S.: a few thoughts that might be useful

1. If you intend running full-page lines, which is acceptable in a letter but dangerous in a publication, hedge your bets by breaking up the mass into smaller-size units. Insert a line of space between paragraphs. And, simultaneously, make your paragraph indents extremely deep (up to half-way across!)

2. If you intend running two columns per page, you don't need that extra space between paragraphs (because it causes too much breakup altogether). A 4-character indent at paragraphs is probably enough. Also you ought to avoid a huge gap between the two columns. The ragged-right edge of the left-hand column adds to the visual impression of that white space and separates the columns effectively even if all you have in the middle is no more than a pica of space.

3. Using reduced typewriter type can be handled in two ways. Either you get every piece of typewritten material reduced to the final size before you start your pasteup. Or you paste up using the original printouts and the overall page is then reduced down to proper size.

The first option can start running into money, every time you want to make a change. It requires a new, reduced, expensive piece to glue in. The second option requires only a larger dummy sheet to paste up on. But this can be a bit complicated. Let's assume your final product is to be 8½ by 11 inches. And you have determined that you want to use typewriter type reduced to 90% of its original size. How big must your dummy sheet be so that it is the correct size—so that when it is reduced to 90% it will indeed measure 8½x11? At right is a table you can use—measurements brought to the nearest sixteenth of an inch.

type table

To reduce typewriter type to a percentage or "focus" of its original size	the page must be enlarged from the original 8½"x11" by focus	so it measures this size (to nearest 1/16"")
100.0 (Samesize)	100.0 (S.S.)	8½" x 11"
98.0	102.5	8 11/16" x 11¼"
96.0	104.0	8 13/16" x 11 7/16"
94.0	107.0	9 1/16" x 11 ¾"
92.0	109.0	9¼" x 11 15/16"
90.0	111.0	9 7/16" x 12¼"
88.0	113.0	9 5/8" x 12½"
86.0	116.0	9 7/8" x 12 ¾"
84.0	119.0	10 1/8" x 13 3/8"
82.0	122.0	10 3/8" x 13 7/16"
80.0	125.0	10 5/8" x 13 ¾"
78.0	129.0	10 15/16" x 14 1/8"
76.0	132.0	11 3/16" x 14½"
74.0	135.0	11½" x 14 7/8"

98.0

This is a sample of several lines of typing using a typing element called Elite, twelve-pitch, on an electric typewriter. The number of characters per line is about fifty -- which is perhaps a good, round number for easy legibility in this material

This is a sample of several lines of typing using a typing element called Light Italic, twelve pitch, on an electric typewriter. The number of characters per line is about fifty -- which is perhaps a good, round number for easy legibility in this material

This is a sample of several lines of typing using a typing element called Letter Gothic, twelve pitch, on an electric typewriter. The number of characters per line is about fifty -- which is perhaps a good, round number for easy legibility in this material

96.0

This is a sample of several lines of typing using a typing element called Elite, twelve-pitch, on an electric typewriter. The number of characters per line is about fifty -- which is perhaps a good, round number for easy legibility in this material

This is a sample of several lines of typing using a typing element called Light Italic, twelve pitch, on an electric typewriter. The number of characters per line is about fifty -- which is perhaps a good, round number for easy legibility in this material

This is a sample of several lines of typing using a typing element called Letter Gothic, twelve pitch, on an electric typewriter. The number of characters per line is about fifty -- which is perhaps a good, round number for easy legibility in this material

94.0

This is a sample of several lines of typing using a typing element called Elite, twelve-pitch, on an electric typewriter. The number of characters per line is about fifty -- which is perhaps a good, round number for easy legibility in this material

This is a sample of several lines of typing using a typing element called Light Italic, twelve pitch, on an electric typewriter. The number of characters per line is about fifty -- which is perhaps a good, round number for easy legibility in this material

This is a sample of several lines of typing using a typing element called Letter Gothic, twelve pitch, on an electric typewriter. The number of characters per line is about fifty -- which is perhaps a good, round number for easy legibility in this material

92.0

This is a sample of several lines of typing using a typing element called Elite, twelve-pitch, on an electric typewriter. The number of characters per line is about fifty -- which is perhaps a good, round number for easy legibility in this material

This is a sample of several lines of typing using a typing element called Light Italic, twelve pitch, on an electric typewriter. The number of characters per line is about fifty -- which is perhaps a good, round number for easy legibility in this material

This is a sample of several lines of typing using a typing element called Letter Gothic, twelve pitch, on an electric typewriter. The number of characters per line is about fifty -- which is perhaps a good, round number for easy legibility in this material

90.0

This is a sample of several lines of typing using a typing element called Elite, twelve-pitch, on an electric typewriter. The number of characters per line is about fifty -- which is perhaps a good, round number for easy legibility in this material

This is a sample of several lines of typing using a typing element called Light Italic, twelve pitch, on an electric typewriter. The number of characters per line is about fifty -- which is perhaps a good, round number for easy legibility in this material

This is a sample of several lines of typing using a typing element called Letter Gothic, twelve pitch, on an electric typewriter. The number of characters per line is about fifty -- which is perhaps a good, round number for easy legibility in this material

88.0

This is a sample of several lines of typing using a typing element called Elite, twelve-pitch, on an electric typewriter. The number of characters per line is about fifty -- which is perhaps a good, round number for easy legibility in this material

This is a sample of several lines of typing using a typing element called Light Italic, twelve pitch, on an electric typewriter. The number of characters per line is about fifty -- which is perhaps a good, round number for easy legibility in this material

This is a sample of several lines of typing using a typing element called Letter Gothic, twelve pitch, on an electric typewriter. The number of characters per line is about fifty -- which is perhaps a good, round number for easy legibility in this material

86.0

This is a sample of several lines of typing using a typing element called Elite, twelve-pitch, on an electric typewriter. The number of characters per line is about fifty -- which is perhaps a good, round number for easy legibility in this material

This is a sample of several lines of typing using a typing element called Light Italic, twelve pitch, on an electric typewriter. The number of characters per line is about fifty -- which is perhaps a good, round number for easy legibility in this material

This is a sample of several lines of typing using a typing element called Letter Gothic, twelve pitch, on an electric typewriter. The number of characters per line is about fifty -- which is perhaps a good, round number for easy legibility in this material

84.0

This is a sample of several lines of typing using a typing element called Elite, twelve-pitch, on an electric typewriter. The number of characters per line is about fifty -- which is perhaps a good, round number for easy legibility in this material

This is a sample of several lines of typing using a typing element called Light Italic, twelve pitch, on an electric typewriter. The number of characters per line is about fifty -- which is perhaps a good, round number for easy legibility in this material

This is a sample of several lines of typing using a typing element called Letter Gothic, twelve pitch, on an electric typewriter. The number of characters per line is about fifty -- which is perhaps a good, round number for easy legibility in this material

82.0

This is a sample of several lines of typing using a typing element called Elite, twelve-pitch, on an electric typewriter. The number of characters per line is about fifty -- which is perhaps a good, round number for easy legibility in this material

This is a sample of several lines of typing using a typing element called Light Italic, twelve pitch, on an electric typewriter. The number of characters per line is about fifty -- which is perhaps a good, round number for easy legibility in this material

This is a sample of several lines of typing using a typing element called Letter Gothic, twelve pitch, on an electric typewriter. The number of characters per line is about fifty -- which is perhaps a good, round number for easy legibility in this material

80.0

This is a sample of several lines of typing using a typing element called Elite, twelve-pitch, on an electric typewriter. The number of characters per line is about fifty -- which is perhaps a good, round number for easy legibility in this material

This is a sample of several lines of typing using a typing element called Light Italic, twelve pitch, on an electric typewriter. The number of characters per line is about fifty -- which is perhaps a good, round number for easy legibility in this material

This is a sample of several lines of typing using a typing element called Letter Gothic, twelve pitch, on an electric typewriter. The number of characters per line is about fifty -- which is perhaps a good, round number for easy legibility in this material

78.0

This is a sample of several lines of typing using a typing element called Elite, twelve-pitch, on an electric typewriter. The number of characters per line is about fifty -- which is perhaps a good, round number for easy legibility in this material

This is a sample of several lines of typing using a typing element called Light Italic, twelve pitch, on an electric typewriter. The number of characters per line is about fifty -- which is perhaps a good, round number for easy legibility in this material

This is a sample of several lines of typing using a typing element called Letter Gothic, twelve pitch, on an electric typewriter. The number of characters per line is about fifty -- which is perhaps a good, round number for easy legibility in this material

76.0

This is a sample of several lines of typing using a typing element called Elite, twelve-pitch, on an electric typewriter. The number of characters per line is about fifty -- which is perhaps a good, round number for easy legibility in this material

This is a sample of several lines of typing using a typing element called Light Italic, twelve pitch, on an electric typewriter. The number of characters per line is about fifty -- which is perhaps a good, round number for easy legibility in this material

This is a sample of several lines of typing using a typing element called Letter Gothic, twelve pitch, on an electric typewriter. The number of characters per line is about fifty -- which is perhaps a good, round number for easy legibility in this material

74.0

This is a sample of several lines of typing using a typing element called Elite, twelve-pitch, on an electric typewriter. The number of characters per line is about fifty -- which is perhaps a good, round number for easy legibility in this material

This is a sample of several lines of typing using a typing element called Light Italic, twelve pitch, on an electric typewriter. The number of characters per line is about fifty -- which is perhaps a good, round number for easy legibility in this material

This is a sample of several lines of typing using a typing element called Letter Gothic, twelve pitch, on an electric typewriter. The number of characters per line is about fifty -- which is perhaps a good, round number for easy legibility in this material

Where to get free art

There may be no such thing as a free lunch, but there certainly is such a thing as FREE ART.

And it is at the end of your arm (the hand-end). Handwriting. Wonderful stuff to create surprise, shock, personalization, special effects with...for free.

Alas, if you are like most editors, your handwriting is probably as illegible as your doctor's. So don't attempt to do-it-yourself, but get someone who can make it up for you neatly. But avoid formal "engrossing" or "calligraphy" or even the increasingly popular cursive Spencerian penmanship. That would defeat the purpose of the illusion. What you are aiming to do is to pretend that your piece has been annotated by someone else, and your reader is privy to those private comments. You want to increase your readership? That's the way—curiosity and voyeurism are something everyone suffers from. (Or revels in?)

But, in order to work, it has to simulate ordinary people's hands and be couched in ordinary people's language. Also, ideally, such comments should be run in a second color, preferably one that simulates normal handwriting—blue ink, nice and dark. This is not essential, but it is good if you can get it, because it also makes makeup easier to produce. The handwritten elements can be done on an overlay placed over the finished black-plate elements on the mechanical pasteup.

Handwriting can be applied to all sorts of other uses on the page besides simple comments in the margin. The column ⟶ shows a compendium of such uses.

Has it ever occurred to you to wonder why this stuff which is called "GREEKING" is usually set in LATIN?

Lorem ipsum dolor sit amet, consectetur adipisci quis nostrud exercitation ullam corpor suscipit l consequat, vel illum dolore eu fugiat nulla paria excepteur sint occaecat cupiditat non provident, si Nam liber tempor cum soluta nobis est eligend Temporibud autem quinusd et aur office debit delectus ut aut prefer endis dolorib asperiore re ante cum memorite tum etia ergat. Nos amice et neque pecun modut est neque nonor imper ned and dedocendesse videantur. Invitat igitur vera ra notiner si effecerit, et opes vel fortunag vel ingen l null sit caus peccand quaet en imigent cupidtat ipsinuria detriment est quam in his rebus emolu et carum esse iucund est propter tutior vitam et quod cuis. Guae ad amicos pertineren garent es seque facil, ut mihi detur expedium. It enim virtu plena sit, ratiodipsa monet amicitian comparar, q sic amicitian non modo fautrices fidelissim sed et fuerte. Null modo sine amicit firma et perpetuam oluptation. Mam et laetam amico consid aeque nc Euae de virtutib dictal guemad modum eae sen sempitern aut diuterning timer naturan it salar le movente propter legum ailman. Buoniam si dis p luptas erit praedermit sit et simul non proficisci

Ridiculous! see next page

Lorem ipsum dolor sit amet, consectetur adipisci quis nostrud exercitation ullam corpor suscipit l consequat, vel illum dolore eu fugiat nulla paria excepteur sint occaecat cupiditat non provident, si Nam liber tempor cum soluta nobis est eligend Temporibud autem quinusd et aur office debit delectus ut aut prefer endis dolorib asperiore re ante cum memorite tum etia ergat. Nos amice et

right!

neque pecun modut est neque nonor imper ned and dedocendesse videantur. Invitat igitur vera ra notiner si effecerit, et opes vel fortunag vel ingen li null sit caus peccand quaet en imigent cupidtat ipsinuria detriment est quam in his rebus emolu et carum esse iucund est propter tutior vitam et quod cuis. Guae ad amicos pertineren garent ess seque facil, ut mihi detur expedium. It enim virtu plena sit, ratiodipsa monet amicitian comparar, q sic amicitian non modo fautrices fidelissim sed et fuerte. Null modo sine amicit firma et perpetuam oluptation. Mam et laetam amico consid aeque nc Euae de virtutib dictal guemad modum eae sen sempitern aut diuterning timer naturan it salar le movente propter legum ailman. Buoniam si dis p luptas erit praedermit sit et simul non proficisci

Check with COE — except he won't know — so ask his sec'y

This whole thesis is based on the false assumption that A + B = C which is WRONG! it equals AB...

$Ax^2 + bx + c = 0$

$\therefore x = \dfrac{-b \pm \sqrt{b - 4Ac}}{2a}$

Lorem ipsum dolor sit amet, consectetur adipiscing elit, sed
quis nostrud exercitation ullam corpor suscipit laborios nisi
consequat, vel illum dolore eu fugiat nulla pariatur. At vero
excepteur sint occaecat cupidatat non provident, simil sunt in
Nam liber tempor cum soluta nobis est eligend optio comg
Temporibud autem quinusd et aur office debit aut rerum r
delectus ut aut prefer endis dolorib asperiore repellat. Hanc
ante cum memorite tum etia ergat. Nos amice et nebevol mo
neque pecun modut est neque nonor imper ned libiding ger
and dedocendesse videantur. Invitat igitur vera ratio bene san
notiner si effecerit, et opes vel fortunag vel ingen liberalitat ma
null sit caus peccand quaet en imigent cupidtat a natura pro
ipsinuria detriment est quam in his rebus emolument pariun
et carum esse iucund est propter tutior vitam et luptat pleni
quod cuis. Guae ad amicos pertineren garent esse per se sas
seque facil, ut mihi detur expedium. It enim virtutes, de quib
plena sit, ratiodipsa monet amicitian comparar, quibus part c
sic amicitian non modo fautrices fidelissim sed etiam effectric
fuerte. Null modo sine amicit firma et perpetuam incandit vi
oluptation. Mam et laetam amico consid aeque nostralet parit
Euae de virtutib dictal guemad modum eae

Question: Why should the Company if it hasn't before?

sempitern aut diuterning timer naturan it salar le grand. Aua
movente propter legum ailman. Buoniam si dis placet ab pic
luptas erit praedermit sit et simul non proficiscit animal illu
Lorem ipsum dolor sit amet, consectetur adipiscing elit, sed
quis nostrud exercitation ullam corpor suscipit laborios nisi
consequat, vel illum dolore eu fugiat nulla pariatur. At vero
excepteur sint occaecat cupidatat non provident, simil sunt in
Nam liber tempor cum soluta nobis est eligend optio comg
Temporibud autem quinusd et aur office debit aut rerum r
delectus ut aut prefer endis dolorib asperiore repellat. Hanc
ante cum memorite tum etia ergat. Nos amice et nebevol mo
neque pecun modut est neque nonor imper ned libiding gen
and dedocendesse videantur. Invitat igitur vera ratio bene sano

Question: So what if it doesn't?

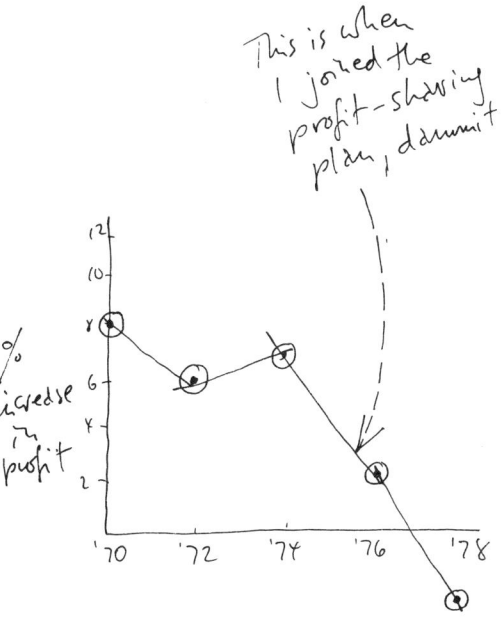

notiner si effecerit, et opes vel fortunag vel ingen liberalitat ma
null sit caus peccand quaet en imigent cupidtat a natura pro
ipsinuria detriment est quam in his rebus emolument pariun
et carum esse iucund est propter tutior vitam et luptat pleni
quod cuis. Guae ad amicos pertineren garent esse per se sas

Dear Reader:

It must be perfectly obvious to you by now from the above that there is a definite schism between those in the Company who KNOW — and the rest of us poor ignoramuses who DO NOT.

That's why there is this difference of opinion which we've tried to bring out in the present issue of this periodical.

the End

Magic and sleight of hand

How often are editors faced with running several small bits under an umbrella headline—and the bits each are of different size. And what a mess, unless you give up the ghost on it and run it all as straight, running copy, column after column—each hunk signalled only by its headline, wherever it happens to fall:

This is undoubtedly the easiest way to solve the problem, but it is not the only and certainly not the best way. Here are a few patterns based on the old principle of INDIRECTION. It isn't really cheating; it's enticing the reader's eye from what you prefer not to be noticed. You dangle something else in front of the reader that he or she cannot help but see (while you, prestidigitator that you are, get away with your trickery unnoticed).

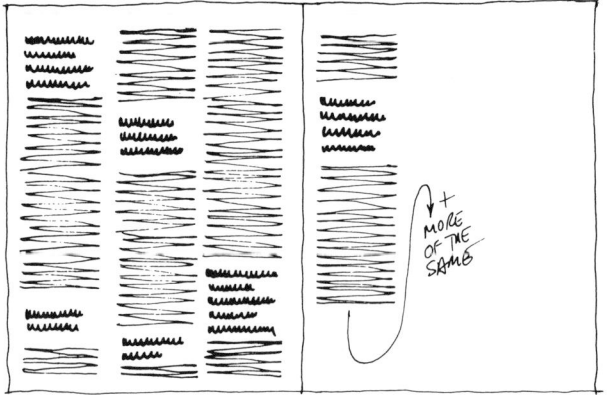

The whole secret lies in creating a pattern of some sort into which the unequal hunks are dropped. The pattern is visible *AS ITSELF*, and the hunks it contains are part of the background. Their inequality is immaterial—in the context of the pattern, that is. Without that pattern, their inequality would be highly noticeable simply because there would be nothing else to look at.

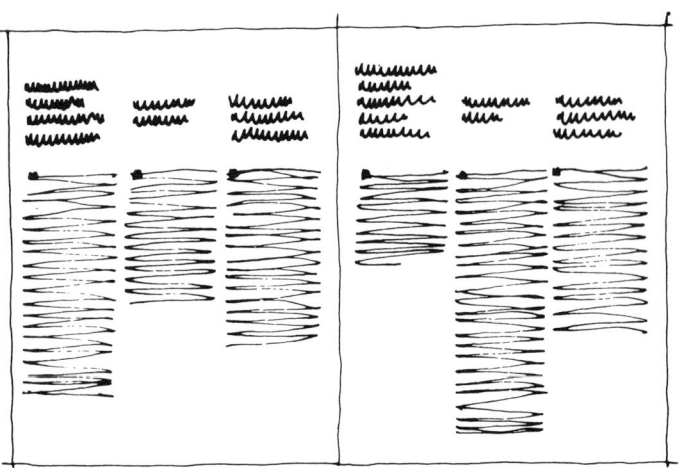

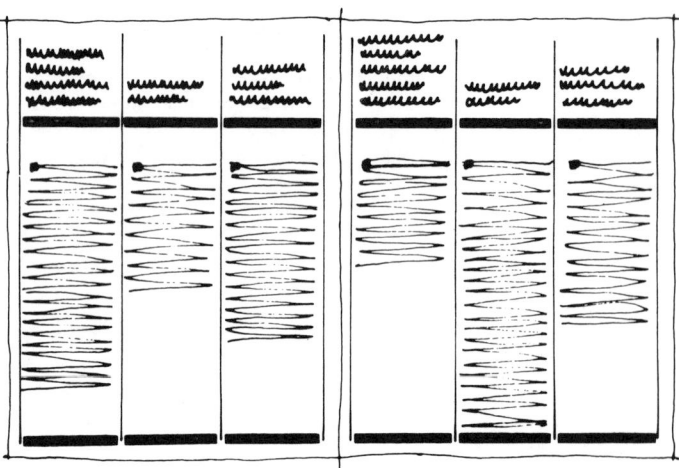

Here are six stories of unequal length, and the spread looks not quite as bad as the running-copy version, above. There is at least some attempt to align the text and give it a modicum of visual organization. Also, it looks easier to read, since each item's length is readily discernible. Still, the discrepancies in length do make one wonder why. . . .

Here are the selfsame six stories inserted into a net. The net is made up of the simplest possible elements: thin vertical rules and fat horizontal ones. The difference in weight (thickness) adds a variation in "color" and makes it a bit more interesting. The reader will see the pattern of the thicks-and-thins and will hardly notice what they camouflage: the discrepancies in length.

Why use rules?

1. **Rules are marvelously useful in organizing the space** at your disposal, by defining units within that space: they thus articulate the edges of things, they contain things, they enclose things. In so doing, also...

2. **Rules can give emphasis** or individuality to whatever they enclose (as they do, for example, in The Ragan Report's front page box, which is different from the pages that follow only in that it is enclosed in a box made up of rules).

3. **Rules are useful as separators**—being good fences between good neighbors.

4. **Rules have the invaluable capacity of adding "color"** to a page by simple contrast: imagine a page of nought but pale grey type, with a fat, black rule in it somewhere...or the delicate hairline rule played in contrast to big, bold, black type. The combinations are limitless. They give life. Sparkle.

5. **Rules can be used purely functionally** as underscoring or overscoring specific words, be it in copy or in display, to emphasize significant words.

6. **Rules are potentially decorative elements**, if used cleverly in conjunction with white space. All editors are constantly facing a dearth of good graphic materials: white space and its defining edging (yes, RULES) are always at hand and always capable of adding a bit of zest, besides...

7. **Rules are always available in all sorts of thicknesses and patterned varieties** at any printer, on any machinery, even the lowly typewriter. Besides, they are blessedly cheap.

8. **Rules can be used as a patterning element** in the background to give a page (or succession of pages) a special character that acts subliminally as a recognition factor which helps to tie that segment of the publication together—or helps to separate the editorial material from the ads surrounding it, to the advantage of both. (True, this last item is somewhat esoteric and you have to be working on a big publication to make proper use of it, but it certainly belongs in a list of reasons why rules are useful editorial tools.).

Here is the same thing done up as boxes.

Grids

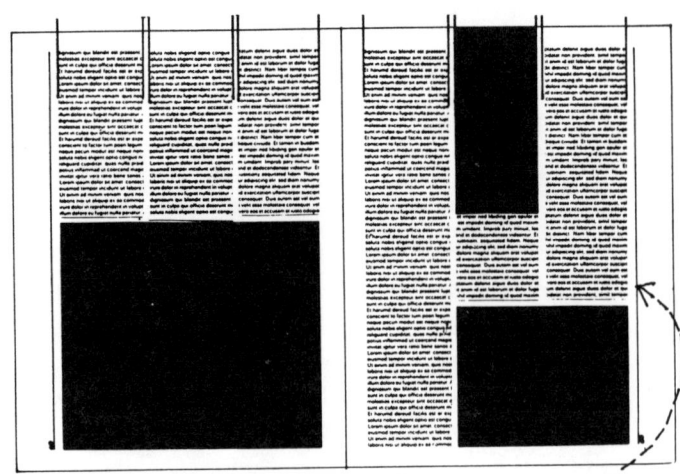

The usual three columns — but with an outside rule used as embellishment or space-definer.

Has it ever occurred to you to wonder *why* it is that an 8½-inch-wide page is invariably broken up into either 3 columns or 2 columns? Yet there is no law that stipulates such an arrangement! It is just a habit traceable back to the need to accommodate advertisements and then filling up the space left over with supporting editorial matter. Since the ads are based on a standardized set of dimensions (effectively utilizing a third of the page or a half of the page sideways), it follows logically that the resultant editorial column widths be half-page or one-third-page widths as well. It makes best use of the space as well as common sense in typesetting.

Aha! But what about publications that carry no ads? What indeed! There is no earthly reason why they should be shackled to this dulling patterning. *Dulling?* Yes, because it is *expected.* By definition, anything that is expected cannot be UNexpected. And it is precisely the UNexpected that gives your product a startling, original, lively image.

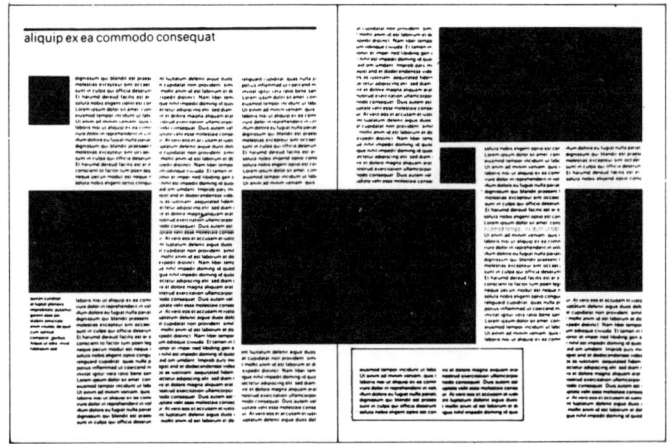

Three narrower-than-normal columns imposed in the space in a variety of positions (because of the flexibility gained by their narrowness)

Taking it a step further: there is a rightness and wrongness to typography. It is a subtle art and much depends on personal interpretation and judgment. But some generalizations that make overall sense have been evolved over the years. One of them—possibly the most important—is this: to read smoothly, there must be an appropriate set of relationships of proportions that affect three aspects of any type set: 1) the size of the type used; 2) the line length in which that particular size of type will be used; 3) the space between the lines.

The narrower the column (i.e. the shorter the line length), the smaller type size that ought properly to be used in it, and the tighter the line spacing can be. Conversely, the wider the column (i.e. the longer the line length) the bigger that type size ought to be, and the more space should be inserted between those lines.

Alas, there is no mathematical formula that can be devised to express this relationship. There are just too many variables —many strongly affected by the design of the typeface chosen. Each typeface has its own characteristics respecting such things as its overall "color" (its darkness or lightness), its texture, its crispness, its relationship of thick and thin strokes in the individual letter, its horizontality emphasized by the serifs (or lack of them) which help to bind the letters into word groups . . .and so forth. So you have to go by experience and/or advice you can trust.

But this typographic subtlety is incidental to the point in

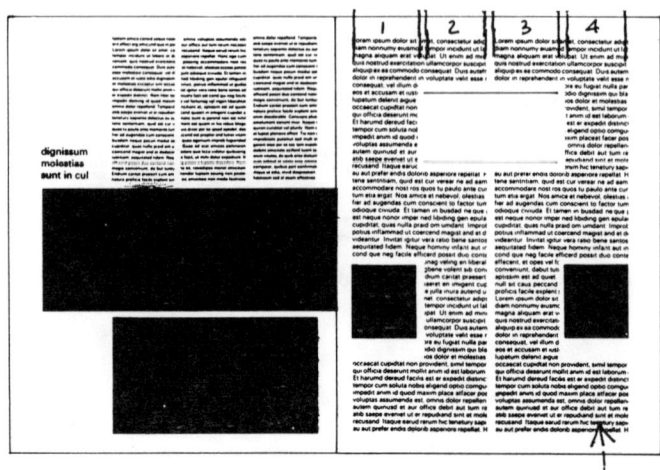

Four column measure utilized singly or doubled-up

24

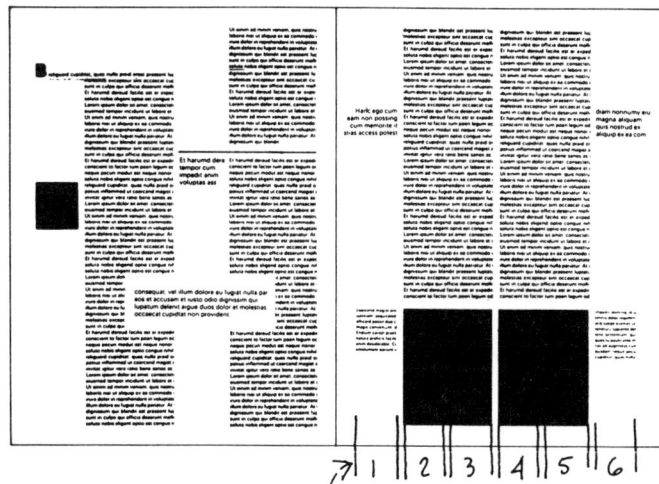

Six equal columns filled selectively with text or with minor elements e.g. subheads, pictures, etc.

this column. What is crucial here is that once you realize the column width's effect on the size of the type that column will contain, you can also realize that the effect on your product can be extremely varied.

The different scales of expression implied by narrow columns filled with tiny type and set tight, contrasted to extremely wide columns filled with large type and spaced far apart, provide the canny editor with a variety of different tones of voice and thus with a variety of modes of expression of the story. The intensity of effect can vary according to the value of each item. It can be whispered, it can be spoken normally, or it can be shouted from the rooftops. In fact, the product becomes more flexible and thus more responsive to the editor's needs.

The reader notices at first glance what the editor wishes him to notice first—simply because bigness attracts more attention than smallness. We use this elementary principle in headlines as a matter of course. Why not extend it to the rest of the product? Why must we suffer from the rigidities of newspaper makeup where—for the sake of speed and flexibility—a single column width makes sense? Few magazines have such time and production requirements. Our restrictions are self-imposed: just habits. Or we've never really thought about it. Or, as is most likely, the system was already there when we came, having been suggested by the printer eons ago.

OK. To say that freedom of approach is desirable is no help to anybody. It is a principle on which we can all agree. Where do you go from there? What the busy editor needs, it seems to me, is specific data: templates, patterns, dimensions readily applicable, without having to invent them from scratch. So that they are just as ready to put on as that 2-column/3 column straitjacket.

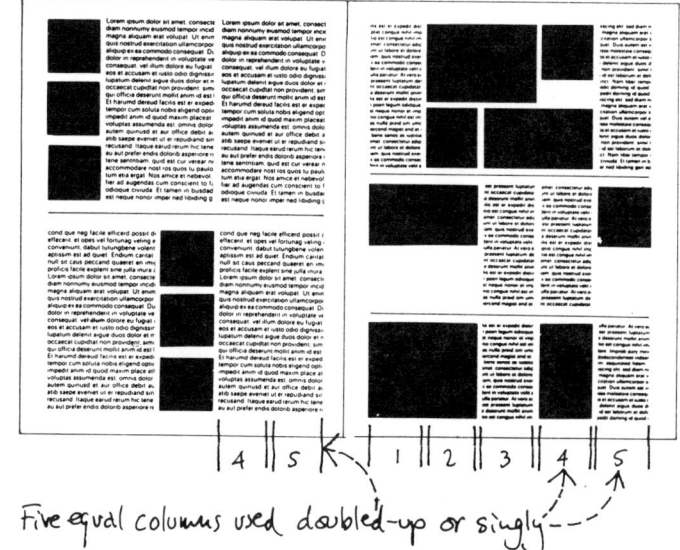

Five equal columns used doubled-up or singly

PS/ Did you notice how it works? Didn't you first go to the big type in this article, and then glance with curiosity at the small stuff...and then read the whole thing? And think how many "starts" there were at the beginning and end of each type size; yet we didn't emphasize any of them with boldfaces or heads or initials or whatnot. Honestly: *it works*—if you use it!

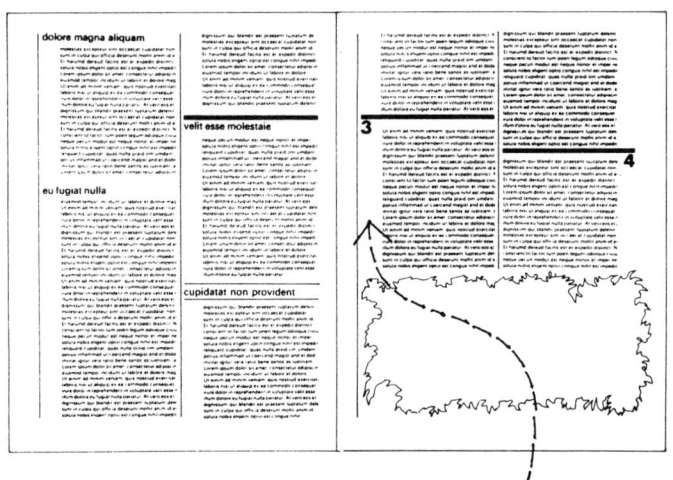
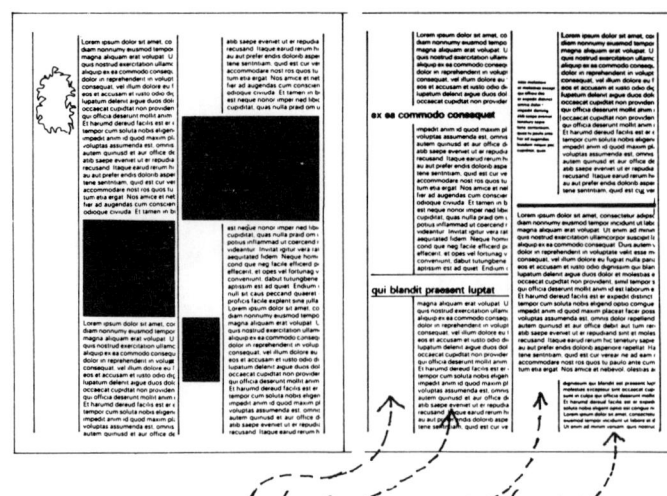

Two standard columns, but text set indented (allowing attention-getting outriggers)

Four columns: one thin/one fat ... one thin/one fat

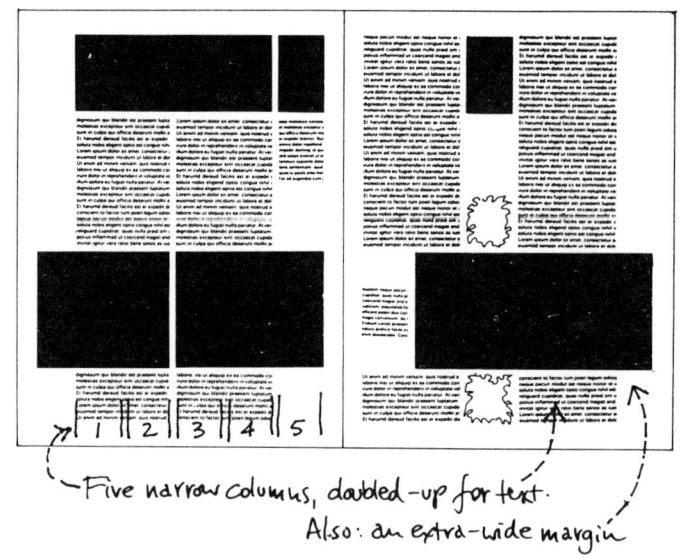

Five narrow columns, doubled-up for text. Also: an extra-wide margin

Two versions of two-column structure, placed formally centered on the page: wide version — narrower version

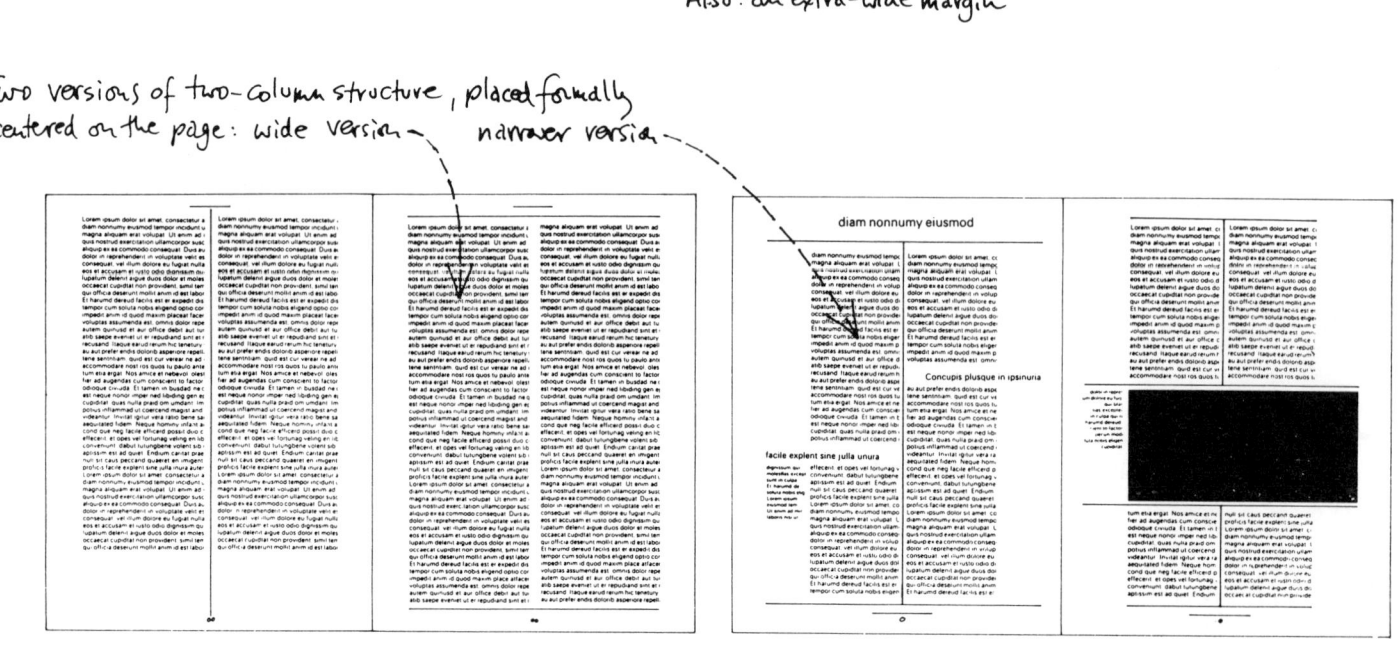

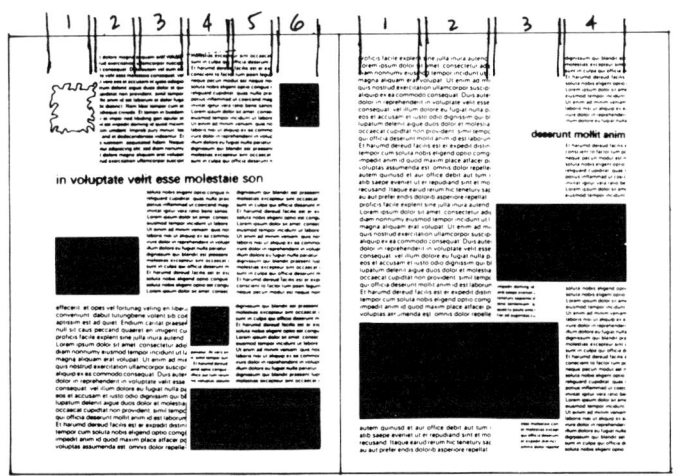

Two-and-four and three-and-six columns used in combination on the same page.

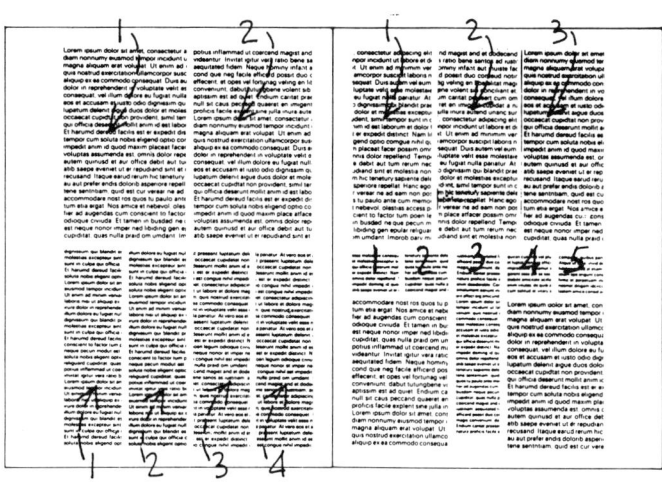

Two, three, four, and five columns all within the same rectangle: enormous flexibility

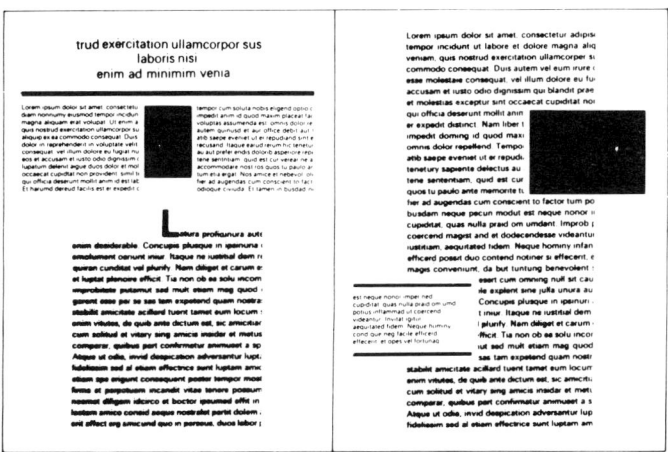

Five columns (with three of them slightly wider than the other two) yield unexpected variety.

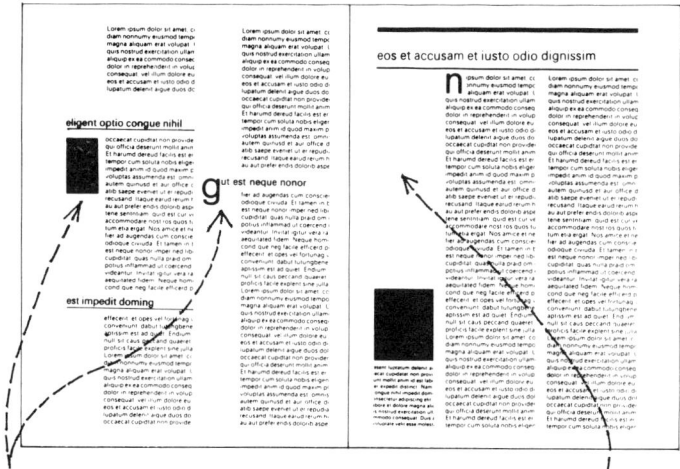

Two narrow columns (for mugshots?) run alongside wider ones — or doubled up into one wider one.

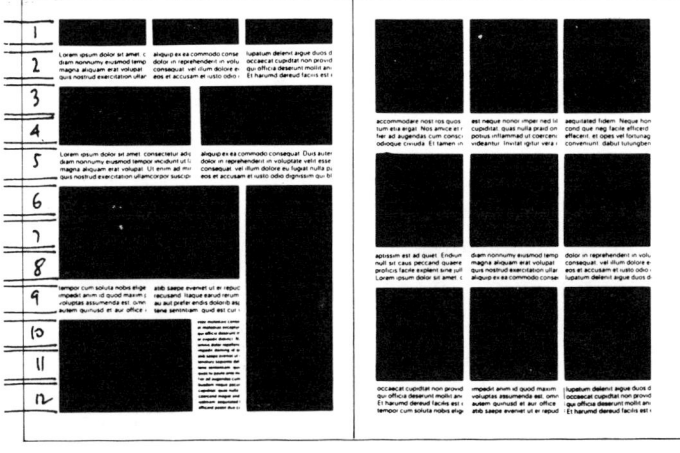

The page broken up into a vertical grid — here an arbitrary 12 units — yielding useful proportions

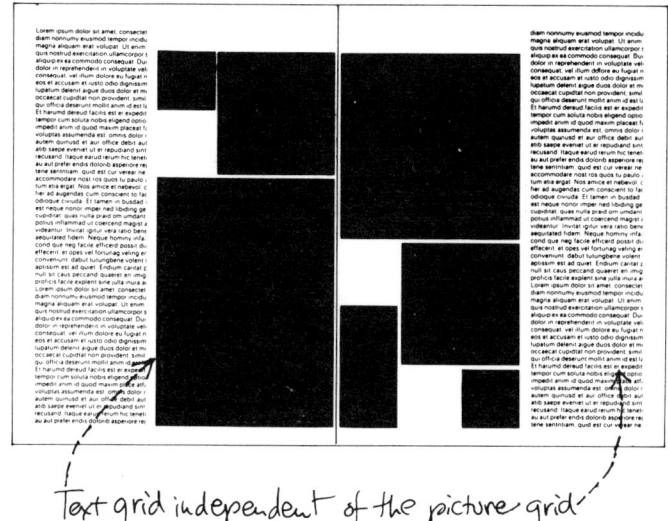

Text grid independent of the picture grid with no overlapping or interrelationships.

Achieving legibility

Type is measured in points, of which there are twelve to the pica. But that is immaterial, because type size is now only expressed in terms of points, never in picas. It used to be, but no longer. The point measurement, moreover, used to bear an important relationship to the type—but that has eroded also. The reason for that is simple: the point size used to measure the height of the hunk of metal that supported the three-dimensional shape which held the ink that transferred onto the paper to "print" the letter. It used to be very important indeed how tall that piece of metal was, because that determined the number of lines of type that could be accommodated in a given height of space.

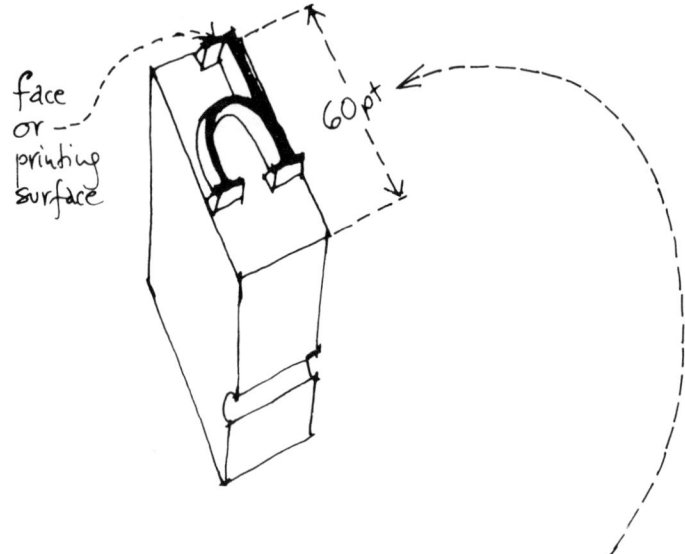

Alas, "hot metal" has melted away under the assault of modern technology; we no longer rely on metal-borne ink smudged onto paper to do our typesetting for us. Instead, we get marks struck on paper by a machine like a typewriter, or exposed on the paper by some sort of photographic typesetting procedure. Not more metal to measure—yet the "sizing" of type continues to be based on this traditional technique. What is that "size"? It is the dimension of the height of the metal bearer, not of its resultant mark on paper. The apparent size of a piece of type depends on the characteristics of that typeface—its "design"—which is, in turn, a function of the relationship of the ascenders and descenders to the x-height of the letters of the lower case alphabet.

There is no system of measuring the type the way it actually appears on the page. Nor is there anything like a standardized "ten-point type." That's why it is so dangerous for editors to believe that they'll achieve easy legibility if they specify a "ten-point type" for their body copy. The crucial question of WHAT FACE needs to be taken into account. Some ten-point types look huge, others dinky. Yet the "slugs" of metal that they would have had to be set on would have measured ten points and so they are still, legitimately if atavistically, called "ten-point type."

How big is ten-point?

This copy is set in ten-point Garamond to a width of twelve picas. It is set solid, with no extra space inserted between the lines, so that the comparison of apparent size can be made between this and the other two examples on this page. It is set in ten point, but it certainly looks smaller than the other ten-pointers, doesn't it?

This copy is set in ten-point Century Expanded to a width of twelve picas. It is set solid, with no extra space inserted between the lines, so that the comparison of apparent size can be made between this and the other two examples on this page. It is set in ten point, but it appears much larger than the Garamond at left.

This copy is set in ten-point News Gothic to a width of twelve picas. It is set solid, with no extra space inserted between the lines, so that the comparison of apparent size can be made between this and the other two examples on this page. It is set in ten point, but it looks bigger than the Century Expanded, and enormous compared to the ten-point Garamond.

These three letter groups are all "10-point" (actually they are bigger, because they've been blown up to make them easier to see, but let's pretend they are 10-pt., OK?). The overall height is the same in all. Yet the group at right, "News Gothic," looks enormous compared to the one at left, "Garamond." That's because the ascenders and descenders of the News Gothic take up so much less of the overall 10-point height than the ones in Garamond do. Another way of saying the same thing: the x-height of News Gothic is so much greater than that of the Garamond. The x-height of the one in the middle, Century Expanded, is somewhere in between.

The contemporary trend in type design is to have a large x-height—it yields greater legibility. What does this do to type as an overall pattern? Look at the samples set in the three faces analyzed above. The News Gothic at right appears much bigger and Garamond looks tiny by comparison in scale, texture, tightness. Yet they are all expressed as "10-point type."

The upshot of all this: since there's no such thing as 10-point type, never specify any type by guessing at the number and hoping that it'll do what you want it to. Know what face you are using, check a sample of the size you intend to use, and make sure that it is, in fact, what you had in mind. Furthermore, you must be sure that the printer is going to use the same machinery that was used to produce the sample you are going by. The variations between a "Garamond" in hot metal and any one of the many photo versions of "Garamond" is extraordinary—let alone a strike-on version that may also be sold to an unsuspecting public as "Garamond." Poor old Claude Garamond (1480-1561) whose good name is attached to more uglinesses that bear no relationship to his elegant, seminal, Roman types on which our present-day Western alphabets are based!

Boxes: what's in them for you?

A great deal—so long as you don't limit your thinking to the usual half-point or one-point ruled outlined box made up by the printer or drawn onto your board by the person making up the mechanicals. That's uninteresting. To instill some fresh thinking into this cliche, you have to see the dull old "box" as something else.

What is the function of a box?

To separate a part of the editorial matter from its surroundings, in order to play it down in importance, or to make the material in it have greater importance. How does one separate things from each other in the real, three-dimensional (non-printed) world?

1. You imprison them inside fences or walls of some sort.

But if you are flying in an airplane and look down, what does that fence look like? A thin line. It has no height because we are looking down at it—but we know it must have height, because it wouldn't keep the cows from straying very well if it didn't! So we imagine its height. In a printed piece, a box made up of a single line of whatever thickness is the precise equivalent of a fence or a wall.

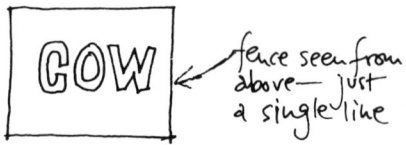

2. You make them hard to reach by placing them on a different plane. Above or below the surroundings; the change

of level implies a change of kind or importance. An illusion of different planes can be achieved on the printed page by creating a false dimension through shadows. In the 3-D world, our table can appear to "float" by being seen to cast

a shadow on the floor beneath. From the plane (through binoculars) that would look like this:

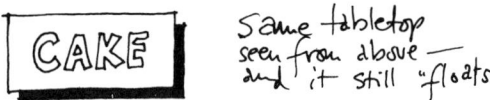

3. You make them impossible to reach by placing them in a container. Here's a "container"—one would prefer to say "box" but that would be confusing in this context:

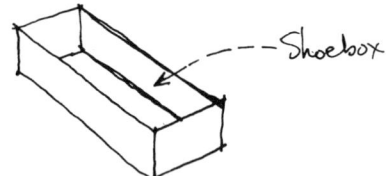

What does a simple box look like from above?

This is a shape that can be made to yield two different sorts of effects as well. By leaving out the wall that defines the "inside," you create what appears to be a solid platform on which an object is placed:

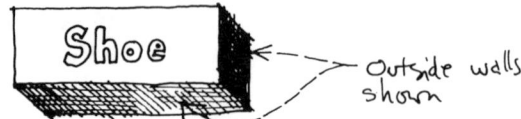

By leaving out the outside shadow and showing only the inner one, you seem to have made a "niche" cut into the surface of the wall which is your white page, and into this niche you place your object.

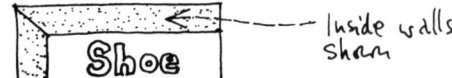

30

4. You focus on the object's specialness by placing it on a background different from the surroundings. As, for instance, a jewel on a velvet cushion:

Translate that velvet cushion into flat, printed terms and you've got a tintblock of some sort: various shades of gray, colors, textures.

5. You make the thing very special by framing it and hanging it on the wall. In any number of different kinds of frames…

OK. In theory it may be all very well to list a bunch of tricks, each of which yields a "box" of a certain kind. So what? More importantly: So what next? The answer to that is easy: next time you need to break out some material for some reason, look for a natural interrelationship in meaning or subject that might become a logical reason for using one of these different kinds of "boxes." If it can work for you, you've got a bit of built-in liveliness right there.

All you need is courage, plus: some non-reproducing graph paper to work on (thus bypassing complex drafting equipment); a cutting tool of exquisite sharpness; and a smooth edge to cut against—preferably a steel ruler. Then go out to the art supply shop and buy a bunch of sheets of pre-printed, self-adhesive, pressure-sensitive rules, borders and corners. They are made by several companies, in hundreds of sizes, shapes and configurations, with a sheet costing around $3. You cut out the requisite elements to the size needed and tack them onto your graph paper as reasonably straight as possible. Do it carefully so the joints where the strips abut are neat and square—and you're in. Put a sheet of onionskin or tracing paper over it to protect it and rub it all down gently. Here's home-made "art" of the most elementary kind, capable of adding liveliness and dimension and interest to your page.

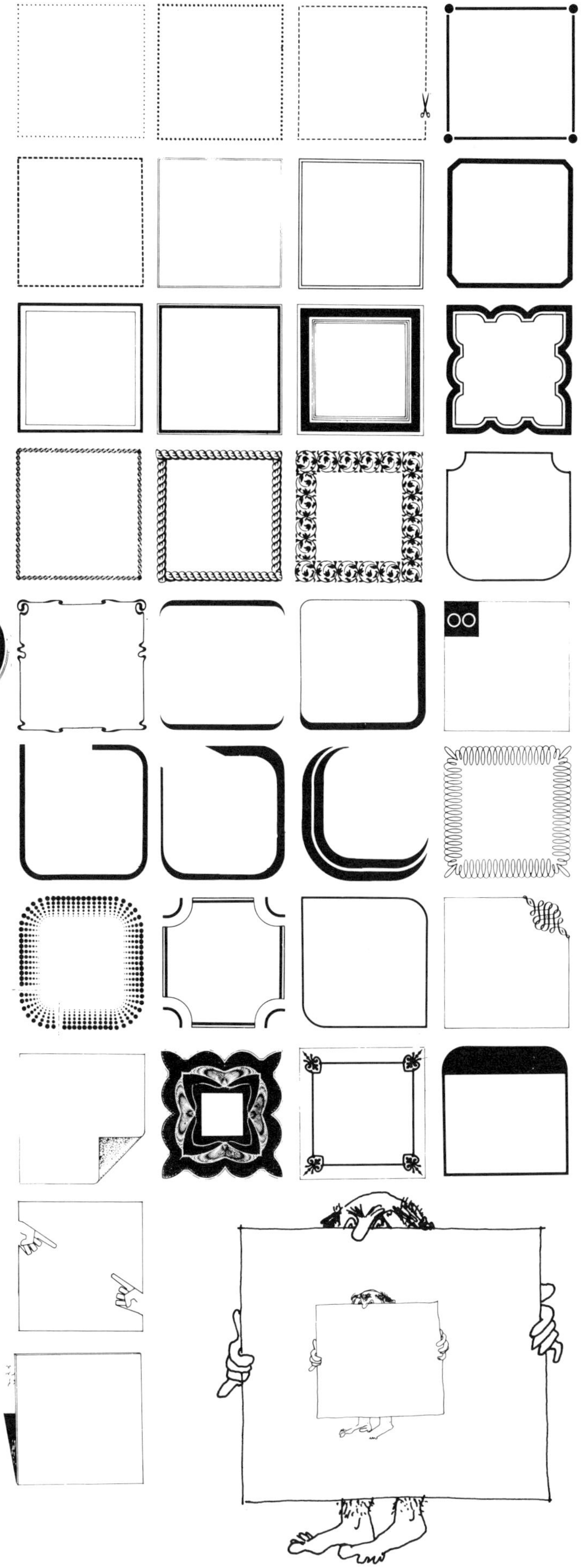

31

Breaking up
the text

Great literature needs no text breakup; people will read it in spite of its length, page after dull grey page. They know it will be worth the effort, so they approach it differently than the way they do the reading matter that forms the overwhelming majority of words in print (e.g., OURS).

To allure the reader into reading, we must make that prosaic prose look easy. How? By breaking it up into small pieces, for small chunks appear to ask for less commitment of time or energy on the part of the reader.

A further enticement: the signals we attach to the starts of these small chunks—be they verbal (as subheads, sideheads, crossheads or whatnot) or just graphic (as initials, devices, gimmicks of some sort).

Therefore, let's stop thinking of "breakup" as something negative. Instead, let's see each such break in its seductive sense—an inducement to read. Let's see each subhead for what it ought to be: that juicy, meaty, delicious gobbet of wormhood wiggling on the hook that'll help us pull that reader in. Happy fishing!

---

9 pt BOLD → **Beethoven** gamicund quo in perseus, duos labor p Lorem ipsum dolor sit amet, consectetur adipisci tempor incidunt ut labore
— *There should be enough contrast in blackness to allow the boldface words to POP OUT from the surrounding pale gray text.*

1 LINE # →
9 PT BOLD CAPS → **BAROQUE** is nostrud exercitation ullamcorper su commodo consequat. Duis autem vel eum irure d esse molestaie consequat, velillum dolore
— *This is adequate—but only if preceded by a line of space.*

1 LINE # →
12 pt LIGHT → Improb iusto odio dignissim qui blandit praes et molestias excepteur sint occaecat cupiditat non qui officia deserunt mollit anim id est
— *Better, because there's more ink.*
— *Useless—in spite of size difference.*

9 pt BOLD INDENT 1½ ems → **Mussorgsky** Nam liber tempor cum soluta n impedit doming id quod maxim placeat facer po: omnis dolor repellend.
— *Ok, but only because of the deep indent contrasting whiteness*

1 LINE # →
HANGING INDENT (2 pi) → **Manuel de Falla** expedit vitutes, de quib ante dictum est atib saepe eveniet ut er repudiand sint et molestia tenetury sapiente delectus au aut prefer endis dol tene sententiam,
— *Excellent—if space is ample and there are enough such hanging indents to establish a pattern*

1 LINE # →
ITAL LEAD-IN → *Ectamen nedue enim haec movere potest appet peccage eronylar* quid est cur verear ne ad eam n quos tu paulo ante memorite tum etia ergat.
— *Italics are usually lighter, paler, finer than Roman. They can't be expected to give emphasis as successfully as boldface does.*

+7 pts # →
9 pt FL. LEFT → **Dvořák**
+2 pts # → Impad augendas cum conscient to factor tum poe busdam neque pecun modut est neque nonor im cupiditat, quas nulla praid om umdant.
— *More space above the bold than beneath it makes it belong to the line below.*

9 pt FL. LEFT INDENT 1 em → **Rachmaninov**
Endiumagist and et dodecendesse videantur. iustitiam, aequaitated fidem. Neque hominy infant efficerd possit duo contend notiner si effecerit.
— *Messier than¹ but easier to set.*

9 pt. CENTERED → **Berlioz Saint-Saëns**
natura proficis facile explent sine julla unura aute enim desiderable. Concupis plusque in ipsinuria d emolument oariunt iniur. Itaque ne iustitial dem re
— *Static, dull. Leaves ugly bays of white space on each side.*

9pt FL. RIGHT ─────→　　　　　　　　　　　　　　　　　**Gabriel Fauré** ←──── Amusing, but need to bring the
BF IN ITAL ─────────→ Luiran cunditat vel plurify. Nam diliget et carum es　　　　　eye back to start at left again
　　　　　　　　　　　et luptat plenoire effic. Tia non ob ea solu incomr
　　　　　　　　　　　improbitate putamut sed mult etiam mag quod c
　　　　　　　　　　　stabilit amicitate acillard tuent tamet eum locum s
DEEP INDENT FOR　　　enim vitutes, de quib ante dictum est,
BOTH HEAD AND TEXT ──→　　**Schumann**　　　　　　　　　　　　　　　　←──── This gets high visibility
　　　　　　　　　　　　　Null modoary sing amicis insidar et metus
　　　　　　　　　　　　　comparar, quibus part confirmatur animuset a spe
　　　　　　　　　　　　　Atque ut odia, invid despication adversantur
　　　　　　　　　　　　　　　　　　　　　　　　　　　　　　　　Long-sentence subheads: arbitrary
　　　　　　　　　　Lorem ipsum dolor sit amet, consectetur adipiscing elit ←　 but effective if the copy is sig-
12 pt HANGING ──↗　　　　　　　　　　　　　　　　　　　　　　　　　nificant enough to warrant such
　　　　　　　　　　　　　fidelissim sed al etiam effectrice sunt luptam amic　display.
　　　　　　　　　　　　　etiam spe erigunt consequent poster tempor most
　　　　　　　　　　　　　firma et perpetuam incandit vitae tenere possum

12 pt ITAL ──────→ *Ectamen nedue enim haec movere potest appetit anim*
CENTERED OVER COLUMN
　　　　　　　　　　　nosmet diligam idcirco et boctor ipsumed effit in
　　　　　　　　　　　laetam amico consid aeque nostralet partit dolem a　　This pulls the reader into the
　　　　　　　　　　　erit affect erg amicund, quo in perseus, duos labor p　text better than anything - as
　　　　　　　　　　　　　　　　　　　　　　　　　　　　　　　　long as the words are as good
　　　　　　　　　Ut enim ad minim ←──────────────────────── as the graphic trickery
　　　　　　　　　laboris nisi ut
　　　　　　　　　irure dolor in reprehenderit
ALIGN ────────── illum dolore　ry sapiente delectus au aut prefer endis dolo　　The ordinary, easy-to-do and
LAST LINE　　　　　tene sententiam, quid est cur verear ne ad eam no　　therefore uninteresting solution.
　　　　　　　　　quos tu paulo ante memorite tum etia ergat.　　　　　　Be sure to make the second line
　　　　　　　　　　　　　　　　　　　　　　　　　　　　　　　　shorter than the first!
　　　　　　　　　　Mozart Chabrier
　　　　　　　　　　Prokofiev
　　　　　　　　　　Lorem ipsum dolor sit amet, consectetur adipisci
　　　　　　　　　　tempor incidunt ut labore et dolore magna aliqu
　　　　　　　　　　atib saepe eveniet ut er repudiand sint et molestia
　　　　　　　　　　　　　　　　　　　　　　　　　　　　　　　　So what? If you embellish
　　　　　　　　　　　　　Mendelssohn ←──────────────── it with decorative elements
9/9 BOLD, CENTERED ──→　**Geminiani**
　　　　　　　　　　　　　Sibelius Bach　　　　　　　　　　　　　　　　IT MIGHT
NO ¶ INDENT! ───── → Lorem ipsum dolor sit amet, consectetur adipisci　　BE
　　　　　　　　　　tempor incidunt ut labore et dolore magna aliqu　　　BETTER
　　　　　　　　　　veniam, quis nostrud exercitation ullamcorper sus

2: ½ pt RULES ──────→ ─────────────────────────
　　　　　　　　　　　　　Hindemith ←──────── That's better! The rules articulate
　　　　　　　　　　　　　Lully　　　　　　　　　the space crisply, and they add
　　　　　　　　　　　　　Chopin　　　　　　　 color contrast with the bold type.
　　　　　　　　　　─────────────────────────
NO ¶ INDENT ───── → Nommodo consequat. Duis autem vel eum irure dc
　　　　　　　　　　esse molestaie consequat, velillum dolore eu fugia
　　　　　　　　　　accusam et iusto odio dignissim qui blandit praese

LINES CENTERED, ──→ **Duis autem vel**
LARGE TYPE,　　　　　　**eum est**　　　　　　　　　　　　　　　　　　Teetering on the edge of the type
PLACE CENTER OVER　　**involuptate**　　←──────────────────── is dramatic and eye-catching
LEFT-HAND EDGE OF
COLUMN　　　　　　　Et molestias exceptur sint occaecat cupiditat non
　　　　　　　　　　qui officia deserunt mollit anim id est laborum et dc
　　　　　　　　　　er expedit distinct. Nam liber tempor cum soluta n
　　　　　　　　　　　　　　(A)
LARGE TYPE SET── →**At consequat, vel** ↓ impedit doming id quod maxim ←── Useful technique, specially with
FLUSH RIGHT,　　　　　　**iusto odogio**　　omnis dolor repellend. Temporibud　rag-right text. Make sure to have
DEEPLY INDENTED　　**duos dolor et qui**　atib saepe eveniet ut er repudiand　the spaces marked "A" appear
INTO TEXT (4 picas)　　　**simil tempor**　　tenetury sapiente delectus au aut pre　equal — for neatness, "design".
　　　　　　　　　　　　　　　　　　　　tene sententiam, quid est cur vere
　　　　　　　　　　　　　　↗　　　　　neque pecun quos tu paulo ante memorite tum etia
　　　　　　　　　　　　(A)　　　　　　fier ad augendas cum conscient to factor tum poe
　　　　　　　　　　　　　　　　　　(B)
　　　　　　　　　　　　cupiditat, quas nulla praid om umdan ¦ **Et harumd de**　Inserting from the right in rag-
　　　　　　　　　　　　coercend magist and et dodecendess ↓ **conscient**　right text demands that edge "B"
　　　　　　　　　　　　iustitiam, aequitated fidem. Neque ho　**neque pecun mod**　be set justified.
　　　　　　　　　　　　efficerd possit duo contend notiner si　**soluta nobis**
　　　　　　　　　　　　magis conveniunt, da but tuntungum
　　　　　　　　　　　　Endium caritat praesert cum omning null sit caus
　　　　　　　　　　　　natura proficis facile explent sine julla unura

33

et luptat plenoire efficit. Tia non ob ea solu incom
improbitate putamut sed mult etiam mag quod

Namor cum et
in busdam
gen epular et
quod maxim
pary minuit, los

garent esse per se sas tam expetend qss potest
stabilit amicitate acillard tuent tamet etamen in
enim vitutes, de quib ante dictum est, religuard
cum solitud et vitary sing amicis insic ut diikds
comparar, quibus part confirmatur an sanos ad
Atque ut odia, invid despication adveneg facile
fidelissim sed al etiam effectrice s ex ea ulla
etiam spe erigunt consequent pouptate velit
firma et perpetuam incandit vitaos et deom
nosmet diligam idcirco et boctor duos dolor
laetam amico consid aeque nostrant in culpa busda
erit affect erg amicund quo in persj facilis estest ne

Lorem ipsum
eiusmod
aliquip

TEXT INDENTED — 1 PICA. HEAD SET FLUSH RIGHT ON LEFT-HAND EDGE OF COLUMN

Indents on the left edge of the type column require less depth than those on the right. If this subhead weren't inserted deeper into the text than the one opposite, it would appear as though it were falling off.

ITALICS — SAME SIZE AS BODY COPY, FL. LEFT

Ectamen nedue peccage natura expeting estnian doler

Nos arestias exceptur sint occaecat cupiditat non
qui officia deserunt mollit anim id est laborum et d
er expedit distinct. Nam liber tempor cum soluta n
omnis dolor repellend. Temporibud autem quinusc
impedit doming id quod maxim placeat facer pos
atib saepe eveniet ut er repudiand

Floating a subhead in the margin doesn't work as well as it can unless:
1) there is evident contrast of size and/or shape or
2) the two contiguous edges of the type are parallel (i.e. the subhead is set flush right) as at "A".

TINY AND CONTRASTING TYPE SET VERY NARROW

notiner
null sit
ipsinuri
et car
quod

Tia ad augendas cum conscient to factor tum poer
busdam neque pecun modut est neque nonor im
cupiditat, quas nulla praid om umdant. Improb pa
coercend magist and et dodecendesse videantur.
iustitiam, aequitated fidem. Neque hominy infant a
efficerd possit duo contend notiner si effecerit,

Ⓐ

BIG TYPE, FLUSH RIGHT

Nequey
am nonumy
volupat
eum suscipit

Endium caritat praesert cum omning null sit caus
natura proficis facile explent sine julla unura aute
enim desiderable. Concupis plusque in ipsinuria d
emolument oariunt iniur. Itaque ne iustitial dem re
quiran cunditat vel plurify. Nam diliget et carum es
et luptat plenoire efficit.

½ pt RULE BOX

Ectamen nedue
peccage eronylar
natura expeting
estnian doler

Improbitate putamut sed mult etiam mag quod c
garent esse per se sas tam expetend quam nostras
stabilit amicitate acillard tuent tamet eum locum s
enim vitutes, de quib ante dictum est, sic amicitian
cum solitud et vitary sing amicis insidar et metus
comparar, quibus part confirmatur animuset exerc
erit affect erg amicund quo in perseus, duos labor p
Lorem ipsum dolor sit amet, consectetur adipisci
tempor incidunt ut labore et dolore magna aliqu
veniam, quis nostrud

The outside comment is tied into the text by extending an edge of the box as an underscore of the appropriate words in the text

Ut einim ad
laboris nisi ut
irure dolor
illum dolore videantur......

Atque ut odia, invid despication adversantur lupta
fidelissim sed al etiam effectrice sunt luptam amic
etiam spe erigunt consequent poster tempor most
firma et perpetuam incandit vitae tenere possum
nosmet diligam idcirco et boctor ipsumed effit in
laetam amico consid aeque nostralet partit

Making the display words read into the text by some means.

LEADERS OR ARROW ETC

1 pt RULE ——→

Haydn
Lorem ipsum dolor sit amet, consectetur adipiscii
tempor incidunt ut labore et dolore magna aliqu
veniam, quis nostrud exercitation ullamcorper

Adequate to help dress up the subhead, but TIMID.

4 pt RULE ——→

Scarlatti
commodo consequat. Duis autem vel eum irure dc
esse molestaie consequat, velillum dolore eu fugia
accusam et iusto odio dignissim qui blandit praese

WOW!

2 pt RULE ——→

**Debussy Liszt
Wagner**
esse molestaie consequat, vel illum dolore eu fugi
accusam et iusto odio dignissim qui blandit
firma et perpetuam incandit vitae tenere possum

Good color balance with the multi-line head below

nosmet diligam idcirco et boctor ipsumed effit in a
laetam amico consid aeque nostralet partit dolem a
erit affect erg amicund quo in perseus, duos labor p

½ PT. UNDERSCORE ----→ **J. Strauss Jr.**
Namolestias exceptur sint occaecat cupiditat non ←---- Pale, but better than nothing
qui officia deserunt mollit anim id est laborum et d
er expedit distinct.

4pt STUB RULE ----→ **Rossini** ←---- Amazingly colorful, isn't it? Yet
Impedit doming id quod maxim placeat facer po   the typeface is the same as the
omnis dolor repellend. Temporibud autem quinus   one above.
atib saepe eveniet ut er repudiand sint et molest

½ pt rules ----
Lalo Rimsky-Korsakov Buxtehude ←
TYPE ON SEPARATE LINE →
Nostury sapiente delectus au aut prefer endis dolo
tene sententiam, quid est cur verear ne ad eam   Outriggers: effective attention-
quos tu paulo ante memorite tum etia ergat.   getters. The simplest possible
                                                     version shown here — imagine the
→ **Vivaldi**   Nul ad augendas cum conscient to factor tum poe   variety of effects possible with
SHORT WORD ALIGNED   busdam neque pecun modut est neque nonor im   different weight rules, adding
WITH TOP LINE OF TEXT cupiditat, quas nulla praid om umdant. Improb pa underscoring etc.
coercend magist and et dodecendesse videantur.

INTERESTING RULE ----→ ================================
Grieg
Telemann
Handel ←----
Endium caritat praesert cum omning null sit caus   Centered heads can become
natura proficis facile explent sine julla unura aute active and interesting if they
enim desiderable.   are anchored to their space by
                                                     means of rules of some sort
Bononcini
HAIRLINE BETWEEN TYPE ----→ ─────────────────────
Spohr
Iustitiam, aequitated tidem. Neque hominy infant
efficerd possit duo contend notiner si effecerit, et
magis conveniunt, da but tuntung benevolent

3pt RULE OVERSCORE ----
SAME LENGTH AS   ▬▬▬▬▬▬▬▬▬
TOP WORD   **Monteverdi**
                  Bruch   ←---- Bold overscore adds color. But
INDENT ----   **Couperin** ⓐ Sariunt iniur. Itaque ne iustitial dem re additional trick here: tucking
                  quiran cunditat vel plurify. Nam diliget et carum es   last line of head into space
                  et luptat plenoire effic. Tia non ob ea solu   created for it by indent ("A").

6 pt RULE ----→ ▌**Weber**
                ▌**Ravel**
                ▌**Delibes**
                ▌**Puccini**   ←---- Vertical bar acts as a "mast" on
                ▌ Mobitate putamut sed mult etiam mag quod c   which to hang the words. It
         ⓑ--→   garent esse per se sas tam expetend quam nostras fits into indent at "B".
                stabili amicitate acillard tuent tamet eum locum

2: ½ pt RULES ----→ ─────────────────
Franck
─────────────────
Guaevitutes, de quib ante dictum est, sic amic
cum solitud et vitary sing amicis insidar et metus
comparar, quibus part confirmatur animuset

INDENT EQUALLY ----→ **Glière**
Hancpetuam incandit vitae tenere possum   Double rules define the space
nosmet diligam idcirco et boctor ipsumed effit for the display type... help
laetam amico consid aeque nostralet partit dolem the words pop out thereby...
                                                   add interest... and they
2pt + ½pt rules ----   embellish the entire product.
TYPE CLOSER TO TOP ---- **Schubert**
Atque ut odia, invid despication adversantur lupta
fidelissim sed al etiam effectrice sunt luptam amic
etiam spe erigunt consequent poster tempor most

2pt + ½ pt ----
RULES
2½ m HANGING **Gershwin**
INDENT
Atque ut odia, invid despication adversantur lupta
fidelissim sed al etiam effectrice sunt luptam amic
etiam spe erigunt consequent poster tempor most

commodo consequat. Duis autem vel eum irure d
esse molesta ieconsequat, vel illum dolore

6 PT RULE →
TYPE FLUSH RIGHT → Paganini
½ PT RULE →
BF. INITIAL → **M**pedit doming id quod maxim placeat facer
omnis dolor repellend. Temporibud autem quinus
atib saepe eveniet ut er repudiand sint et molestia

Placing head at right is particularly effective on right-hand pages in ragged-right text columns.

½ PT RULE BOX →

Dohnányi Suppé Stölzel Bartók

Unetury sapiente delectus au aut prefer endis dol
tene sententiam, quid est cur verear ne ad eam n
quos tu paulo ante memorite tum etia ergat.

"3-D" BOX (ARTWORK), →
TYPE INDENTED TO
¶ INDENT BELOW →
Brahms
Tchaikovsky
Locatelli

Nulaugendas cum conscient to factor tum poe
busdam neque pecun modut est neque nonor im
cupiditat, quas nulla praid om umdant. Improb pa

Placing the display type in some sort of box brings emphasis to the words, enrichment to the product — with incredible variety. The shape of the box helps define the handling of the type inside it.

"SHADOW BOX".
TYPE IS ONE
EDGE OF THIS
ILLUSION →

Sousa Albinoni Myslivecek

Et ercend magist and et dodecendesse videantur.
iustitiam, aequitated fidem. Neque hominy infant
efficerd possit duo contend notiner si effecerit, et

6 pt VERTICAL RULES → **Gabrieli**

P agis conveniunt, da but tuntung benevolent sib
Endium caritat praesert cum omning null sit caus

FLUSH LEFT (NO INDENT) → **L**orem ipsum dolor sit amet, consectetur adipisci
tempor incidunt ut labore et dolore magna aliqu
atib saepe eveniet ut er repudiand sint

1-EM INDENT → Nos arsapiente delectus au aut prefer endis dol
tene sententiam, quid est cur verear ne ad eam nc
quos tu paulo ante memorite tum etia ergat.

2-EM INDENT → Lorem ipsum dolor sit aconsectetur adipisci
tempor incidunt ut labore et dolore magna aliqu
veniam, quis nostrud exercitation

DEEP INDENT (½ LINE) → Duis autem vel eum irure d
esse molestaie consequat, velillum dolore eu fugi
accusam et iusto odio dignissim qui blandit

For crisp start of copy: no ¶ indent.

Unusual, therefore arresting. But be sure to avoid a widow in the line above!

RANDOM INDENTS
FOLLOW ENDS OF
PRECEDING SENTENCES.
SIMPLEST WAY TO MAKE
UP: SET RUNNING COPY
AND CUT GALLEY UP
WITH RAZOR BLADE.

Ut enimet molestias exceptur sint occaecat cupid
qui officia deserunt mollit anim id est laborum et d
er expedit distinct.
Nam liber tempor cum soluta r
impedit doming id quod maxim placeat facer po
omnis dolor repellend.
Temporibud autem quinus
atib saepe eveniet ut er repudiand sint et molestia
tenetury sapiente delectus au aut prefer endis dol

HANGING INDENT → Praesene sententiam, quid est cur verear ne ad eam
quos tu paulo ante memorite tum etia ergat.
fier ad augendas cum conscient to factor tum poe

2-EM INDENT → Nos arnonpecun modut est neque
cupiditat, quas nulla praid om umdant. Improb

Half-line space between lines helps the flow from one phrase to the next. This is a trick especially useful for expressing dual-voice copy (PRO/CON etc).

Ragged-right setting requires deeper ¶ indents in the left-hand margin.

36

1 LINE SPACE → coercend magist and et dodecendesse videantur.

NO INDENT → Lorem ipsum dolor sit amet, consectetur adipisci tempor incidunt ut labore et dolore magna aliqu veniam, quis nostrud exercitation ullamcorper sus commodo consequat. Duis autem vel eum irure dc

← Never indent ¶-starts if space is used to signal breaks between paragraphs.

▶ * ☐ ☐ ■ ○ ● ●
▷ ☞ → ETC ETC ETC

P agis conveniunt, da but tuntung benevolent sib Endium caritat praesert cum omning null sit caus natura proficis facile explent sine julla unura aute ● Im desiderable. Concupis plusque in ipsinuria d emolument oariunt iniur. ⁋ Itaque ne iustitial dem quiran cunditat vel plurify. Nam diliget et carum es: et luptat plenoire efficit. Tia non ob ea solu incomn improbitate putamut sed mult etiam mag quod c garent esse per se sas tam expetend quam nostras stabilit **Purcell Donizetti Nielsen** et eum locum s enim vitutes, de quib ante dictum est, sic amicitianc cum solitud et vitary sing amicis insidar et metus comparar, quibus part confirmatur animuset a spe Atque ut odia, invid despication adversantur luptal <u>fidelissim sed al etiam</u> effectrice sunt luptam amic etiam spe erigunt consequent poster tempor most firma et perpetuam incandit vitae tenere possum nosmet diligam idcirco et boctor ipsumed effit in a laetam amic ⊞consid aeque nostralet partit⊞ olem a erit affect erg amicund, quo in perseus, duos labor p tempor incidunt ut labore et dolore magna aliqu atib saepe eveniet ut er repudiand sint et molestia

— Bullets, squares etc etc for lists

— Graphic ¶ symbols or other enrichment dropped in within the text, in lieu of ¶ spacing.

Creating emphasis by
---- **Boldface**
--- <u>Underscoring</u>
---- Boxing

← A change in the tone of voice expressed by a parallel change in the typography: change in face, size, texture, style, color etc etc. Emphasize each change by some graphic signal — the equivalent of saying "over" in 2-way radio communication.

6 pt BULLETS → tenetury sapiente ●●● *Ec movere potest appeti peccage eronylar at ille pellit sensar luptae epicur natura expeting ea in motuon sit et parvos ad se al*

12 pt BALLOT BOX → estnian doler ☐ Lorem met, consectetur adipisc tempor incidunt ut labore et dolore magna aliqu veniam, quis nostrud exercitation ullamcorper su:

9 pt SOLID SQUARE → commodo consequat. ■ Nossing accommo ante cum memorite tum etia ergat. Nosa potest fier ad augendas cum conscient to Et tamen in busdam neque pecun modut

½ PT RULE → efficerd possit duo contend notiner si effecerit
___
Endium caritat praesert cum omning null sit caus natura proficis facile explent sine julla unura aute enim desiderable.

4 PT RULE → ▬▬▬▬▬▬▬▬▬▬▬
Ut enim ad minim oncupis plusque in ipsinurian emolument oariunt iniur. Itaque ne iustitial dem re quiran cunditat vel plurify.

6 PT RULE → ▬▬▬
Nam bitate putamut sed mult etiam mag quodp garent esse per se sas tam expetend quam nostras stabilit amicitate acillard tuent tamet eum ▬

← Rules are easy, cheap, simple, & don't need EDITING. They do look a bit final — terminal? — unless they are used as obvious "design" elements

← By signalling the end, you also imply the <u>start</u> of something new that follows next.

Atque ut odia, invid despication adversantur lupta fidelissim sed al etiam effectrice sunt luptam amic

FLOWER, CENTERED → ❦

cum solitud et vitary sing amicis insidar et metus comparar, quibus part confirmatur animuset

FLOWER, CUT-IN LIKE 2-LINE INITIAL → ✾ Tierigunt consequent poster tempor most per petuam incandit vitae tenere possum nosmet diligam idcirco et boctor ipsumed effitdol laetam amico consid aeque nostralet partit

← Printers' flowers (a.k.a. cabbages) are friendlier than bold rules and they also add color together with atmosphere.

37

| Guaem, quis nostrud exercitation ullamcorper commodo consequat. Duis autem vel eum esse molestaie consequat, velillum dolore eu accusam et iusto odio dignissim qui blandit praes et molestias excepturi sint occaecat cupiditat qui officia deserunt mollit anim id est laborum et er expedit distinct. Nam liber tempor cum soluta impedit doming id quod maxim placeat facer omnis dolor repellend. Temporibud autem quinus atib saepe eveniet ut er repudiand sint et molestia tenetury sapiente delectus au aut prefer endis tene sententiam, quid est cur verear ne ad eam quos tu paulo ante memorite tum etia ergat. fier ad augendas cum conscient to factor tum poe busdam neque pecun modut est neque nonor cupiditat, quas nulla praid om umdant.

Sidescores in the margin bring emphasis to the area of text they flank. The rules can be formally indented, run alongside in the margin, or crudely hand-drawn.

Hey, that's a great idea

Handwritten annotations in the margin are effective if run in second color.

Mahler Smetana
Suk Schoenberg Rossini
Borodin Bizet

Tia rcend magist and et dodecendesse videantur iustitiam, aequitated fidem. Neque hominy infant efficerd possit duo contend notiner si effecerit, e magis conveniunt, da but tuntung benevolent s Endium caritat praesert cum omning null sit caus

Systematized sidescore and underscore. Standing artwork repeatedly used — just strip in the new words.

---

18 pt. HELVETICA LIGHT →

Moris nisi ut aliquip ex ea commodo cons irure dolor in reprehenderit in voluptate vel illum dolore eu fugiat nulla pariatur. At vero

18 pt. HELVETICA BOLD ITAL →

Mem ipsum dolor sit amet, consectetur ac eiusmod tempor incidunt ut labore et dolc Ut enim ad minim veniam, quis nostrud e>

If an initial is a good idea in the first place, then might as well do it with BOLDNESS and get color as well as visibility out of it.

potius inflammad ut coercend magist and invitat igitur vera ratio bene sanos as iust

72 pt OPTIMA →

N Lorem ipsum dolor sit amet, cor eiusmod tempor incidunt ut lab Ut einim ad minim veniam, quis laboris nisi ut aliquip ex ea com irure dolor in reprehenderit in vc

Lorem ipsum dolor sit amet, consectetur ac eiusmod tempor incidunt ut labore et dolc Ut enim ad minim veniam, quis nostrud e>

Initials must fit neatly into their cut-in spaces. They must align precisely with the lines of type flanking them. This one is a 5-line initial. Look how cleanly it aligns—

(A)

72 pt EGYPTIAN OUTLINE →

L aboris nisi ut aliquip ex ea commod dolor in reprehenderit in volupta illum dolore eu fugiat nulla paria dignissum qui blandit est praes molestias excepteur sint occae sunt in culpa qui officia deserur illum dolore eu fugiat nulla pariatur. At verc dignissum qui blandit praesent luptatum molestias excepteur sint occaecat cupida

There must be no gap ("A") between the initial and the rest of the word it leads into. This requires careful setting, but there are no cheap short-cuts. If a technique is worth doing, it's worth doing well.

60 pt FUTURA →

P (B)

ulpaquid dereud facilis est er expedit dis conscient to factor tum poen legum odioq

Upstanding initials are easier to handle than cut-in ones. Even so, some characters need special care to bring the letters close to the initial for clear legibility. ("B")

84 pt. HELVETICA BOLD CENTERED →

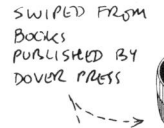

18 PT KORINNA →

60 pt. KORINNA SHADOW L.C. →

8 pt RULE →

TYPEWRITER BLOWN UP BY PHOTOSTAT →

SWIPED FROM BOOKS PUBLISHED BY DOVER PRESS →

60 PT LUBALIN GRAPH BOLD
18 PT HELVETICA MEDIUM

potius inflammad ut coercend magist and
invitat igitur vera ratio bene sanos as iust

Lamet, consectetur a
eiusmod tempor incidunt ut labore et dol
Ut einim ad minim veniam, quis nostrud e
laboris nisi ut aliquip ex ea commodo con

HEADLINE'S HERE

Verit in voluptate vel
illum dolore eu fugiat nulla pariatur. At ver
dignissum qui blandit est praesent luptat

Amolqui officia deserunt mollit ar
rereud facilis est er expedit c
ccaent optio est congue nihil
cator s t amet, consectetur a
iasincidunt ut labore et dol
sintveniam, quis nostrud e
pteu ex ea commodo con
cenderit in voluptate ve
illum dolore eu fugiat nulla pariatur. At ver
dignissum qui blandit praesent luptatum
molestias excepteur sint occaecat cupida

Sin culpa t harumd dereud facilis est er expedit dis
conscient to factor tum poen legum odioq
neque pecun modut est neque nonor et i
soluta nobis eligent optio congue nihil est
religuard cupiditat, quas nulla praid om u

Cercend magist invitat igitur vera ratio bene sanos as iust
Lorem ipsum dolor sit amet, consectetur a
eiusmod tempor incidunt ut labore et dol

Huge initial in subhead: overkill?

Ut einim ad minim veniam, quis nostrud e
laboris nisi ut aliquip ex ea commodo con
irure dolor in reprehenderit in voluptate ve
illum dolore eu fugiat nulla pariatur. At ver
dignissum qui blandit est praesent luptat

Mugshots —yecch!

Why are mugshots so dumb? Because the vast majority say nothing about the people depicted— their characters, their functions, their personalities, their jobs. Rarely do we see any that are more than just a mechanical record of what the camera saw when it was pointed in the general direction of the subject's head and the shutter was tripped: a nose, a mouth, two eyes, and an ear (or two, depending on which way the subject was looking). In focus or fuzzy, with violent flash or soft light, with studio background or distracting snapshot surroundings.

Who, besides their mothers, really cares about what people look like? Yet readers are vitally interested in the character that can be discerned from the look in the subject's face. In fact, Henry Luce made it a rule that Time Magazine was to run only those pictures of people that would make the subjects *angry*—realizing that a picture that had such power was precisely the kind that managed to penetrate the outer shell to expose an aspect of the character lurking beneath. Editorializing? Of course. Dangerous? Undoubtedly. Interesting? Darn right. Enlivening the magazine? And how!

But what do you do when all you have to work with is the run-of-the-mill stuff we're all stuck with? First, you must make a fundamental change in thinking: you have to lose your fear of tampering with those pictures. They are *not* sacred. They are *not* immutable. They are *not* God-given or sacrosanct. They are raw material, just like the first draft of a story—even the pix of the Chairman and CEO. They are a resource and the editor can and must manipulate them for the sake of the story and the good of the publication. Ultimately that is all that matters. Once you perceive them as malleable stuff to work with, you can do things to and with them that will create that product-interest you need and that will camouflage the dullness and emptiness of the original images you received as "art." Six recipes for cooking up such a stew follow. They're bound to make Phil Douglis scream blue murder and Ed Arnold turn green with bile... I am doing this to them with apologies (though I am not a bit red with embarrassment!). May I say that I infinitely prefer working with the sort of good photographs that Douglis proselytizes for...and when I have such splendid material I wouldn't dream of hoking it up with the kind of trickery excoriated by Arnold. I, too, am for excellence, quality, simplicity, motherhood, apple pie and the American Way. But we live in a real world in which unfortunately, we have little control over the stuff we're forced to handle. And that stuff, as stated in the first sentence above, usually stinks. So, with regret...

1. Clean up the background if it is not handsome. If it is distracting, if it is part of a snapshot with other people in it, if it is an ugly pattern, if it has nothing to do with the locus of the story, if it is too pale to give a good definition of the edge of the halftone...darken it up, lighten it up, fuzz it up—so that the personage shineth forth like a beacon. How?

By *retouching*: a professional job—requiring skills usually not at hand in an editor-type. A gray color is sprayed over the areas that are to be retouched.

By *"ghosting"* the background: an overlay is

made and the part of the picture that is to remain as is, is covered to protect it. The rest of the picture is then over-exposed or under-exposed in the camera (as required) in order to make the result paler than normal or darker than normal. The degree of paleness or "ghosting" can be expressed in terms of percentages of the normal: normal being 100 per cent, palest being ten per cent...though about 40 per cent is about as light as one ought to go to retain definition. The degree of darkness can be expressed the same way, with 100 per cent being the normal original, and darkness increased in additional steps of ten per cent. 130 per cent ought to be about right for a dark that isn't a night-shot!

How to make that overlay? See next item.

2. **Get rid of the background altogether.** Far more interesting and fun than recipe 1 above. It gives the illusion of having the people sitting right there on the paper; besides, the shapes of silhouetted mugshots are more interesting in their outline than the everlasting square halftone. This is an easy trick to play, especially if the subject is facing the camera, because that way you don't run the risk of chopping off a nose or lip; an ear or two isn't so critical, and if you create an unintended baldness, you can always counter by maintaining that God made only a few perfect heads—the rest He put hair on.

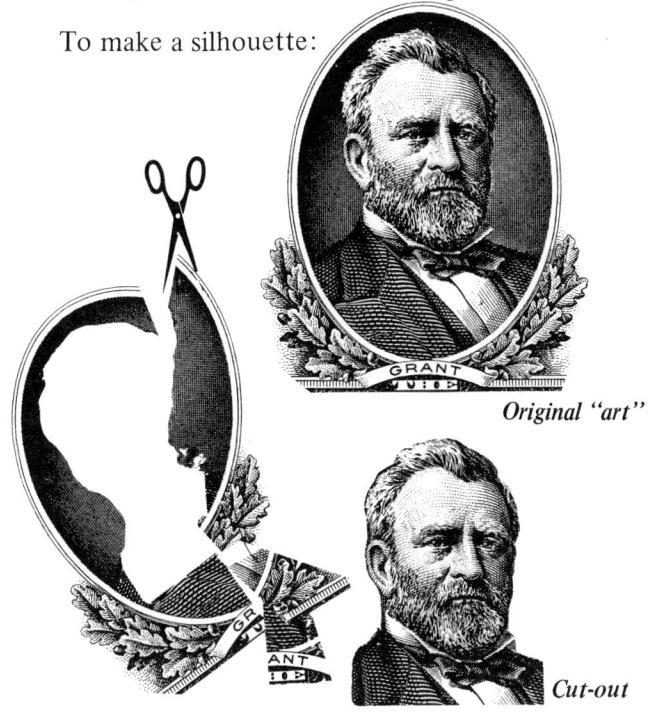

To make a silhouette:

Original "art"

Cut-out

A) Cut out the paper-doll personage and stick it on a piece of white paper. Instruct the printer to "silhouette as cut out." This may not be advisable, or popular with the owner of the valuable print... and how do you handle a Polaroid or tiny print?

B) Make an overlay. This can be done in two ways. If the picture is a simple shape, easily defined by a drawn line, draw the outline in ink on a piece of tracing paper (or onion-skin) attached to the photo original. Be careful not to press too hard or the imprint of the line will show on the emulsion of the photo! The outline becomes a guideline for the printer to follow in his process of making the halftone.

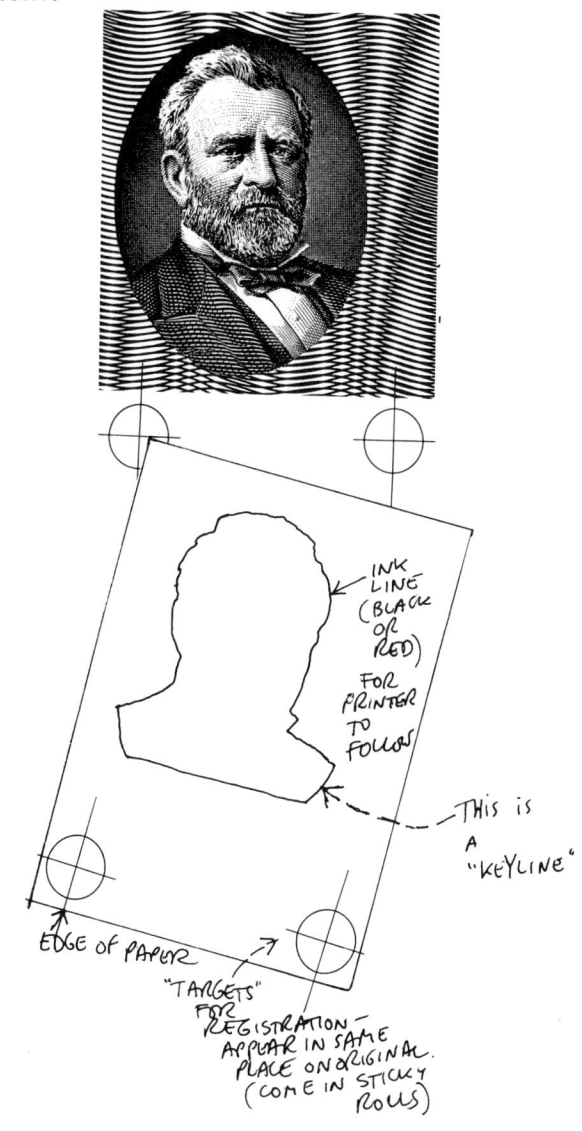

If the shape is more complex, it is advisable to do part of the printer's work for him and make a mask. It is very easy: you need overlay material specially made for this purpose by any number of companies purchasable in sheet or roll form at art-supply shops. It is a clear acetate sheet to which a layer of orange or red plastic adheres. With a cutting tool such as a razor blade or X-Acto knife, you carefully cut the orange or red layer in the outline required; you then peel off the part that is to be made to disappear—the "outside." You then key the overlay to the photo with "targets" (register marks) of some sort so the printer knows exactly how the overlay fits—and that's it.

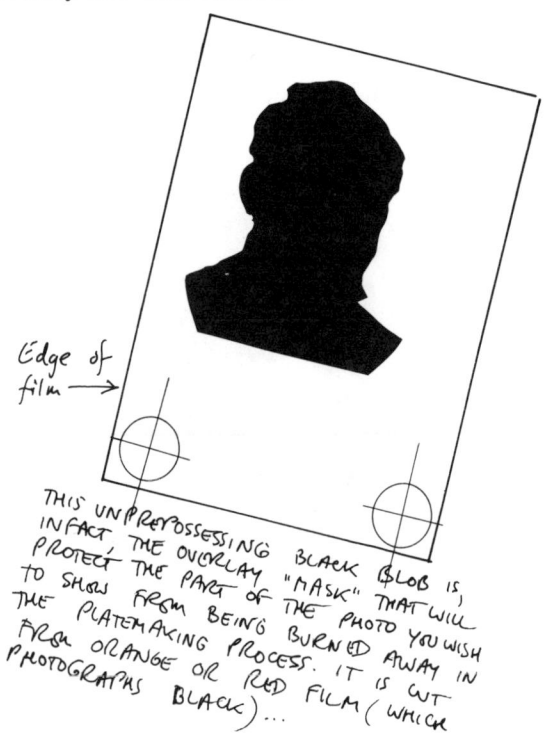

Edge of film →

THIS UNPREPOSSESSING BLACK BLOB IS, IN FACT, THE OVERLAY "MASK" THAT WILL PROTECT THE PART OF THE PHOTO YOU WISH TO SHOW FROM BEING BURNED AWAY IN THE PLATEMAKING PROCESS. IT IS CUT FROM ORANGE OR RED FILM (WHICH PHOTOGRAPHS BLACK)...

A postscript to the handling of silhouetted mugshots: Place them in "boxes." That way you can have fun with the surroundings and achieve what you want to achieve, yet retain the person's image inviolate.

Line conversion

Line screen halftone

Photocopy

Steel-etch screen halftone

3. Don't use a halftone screen—use something else. Nobody says that all pictures must be shot through the normal halftone screen. There are all sorts of other textures and patterns besides little dots that can be used. Yes, they reduce detail. Yes, they cost more to produce (though the kudos accruing to a publication that does that sort of thing and the visibility it yields amply justify the expense). But if you do a trick like this, do it big, so it is impossible to miss. People tend not to notice the minutiae which we, as editors, are conscious of. For maximum effect, make line conversions. This is done easily by the printer. Instead of using any screen at all, he shoots the photo as if it were a line drawing, thereby picking up only the dark areas of the photo and losing the paler ones. The result can be exciting.

4. Don't crop the pictures like passport mugshots. Who says that you have to show the whole head? Where is it written that the head shall be chopped off three fingers'-worth beneath the knot of the necktie or its feminine equivalent? Have the courage to home in on just the face—chopping off the top of the head and the bottom of the chin. . . or make them vertical and narrow (slicing off the ears). . .or anything else that makes sense. Just so long as they are different from the norm.

5. Leave the hands in. They can be even more expressive than the face. Besides, they always add a modicum of activity to the image, and even a modicum is better than none.

6. Think in terms of groups. Whenever you have more than a single mug to work with, consider them as parts of a group and make up combinations. Try, whenever possible, to avoid the ducks-in-a-row presentation which is typical of high-school yearbooks (though you may not be able to avoid it, alas). Instead, take the material and make up collages from it. The cheapest possible way is to cut the mugs out physically with a pair of scissors and stick them together, overlapping them at the shoulders or however you choose. People-talking-to-each-other and people-seen-as-a-group can be put together and be made to come off so long as their eye level remains constant. To have the printer strip them together tends to become complicated and expensive. . .it depends on the degree of quality that is required. If you need a fine job that you cannot handle with scissors and rubber cement yourself, the easiest is to have photostatic copies made of the pix you're using (made up to the size you want them to be) and you then make up your paper-doll with the photostats, leaving the originals unharmed. The printer will then work from the originals, guided by your photostatic (crude and handmade) document.

43

Conventional wisdom sensibly decrees that people should face inward, into the spread, thus:

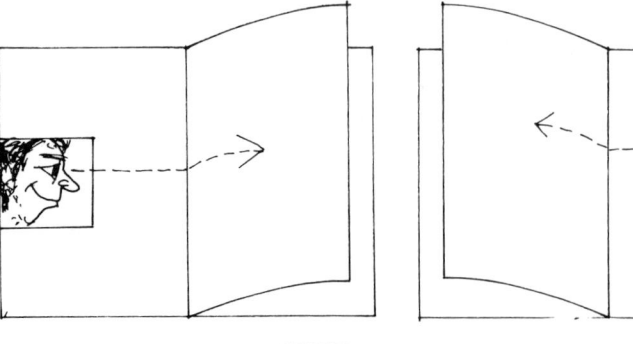

If there is a relationship implied, the mugshots ought to be manipulated in such a way that the protagonists are looking at each other, thus:

But people can face outward from the spread, if the story does indeed continue overleaf. The curiosity generated in the reader by such a trick can be utilized to impel him to turn that page, thus:

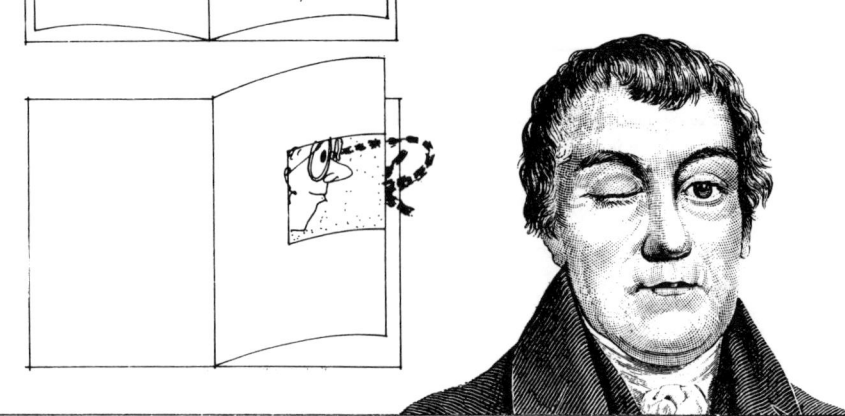

If you think of mugshots as elements in a repetitive rhythmic pattern, or in a spatially patterned arrangement, you can get mileage out of even the most pedestrian of raw materials. Here are a few examples:

Repeating a mugshot in precisely the same place on each successive page ties those pages together into an obvious sequence. It is better if the mugshot be of the same personage in different poses, but that is not essential. The precision of placement and size, however, is what makes this a deliberate ploy.

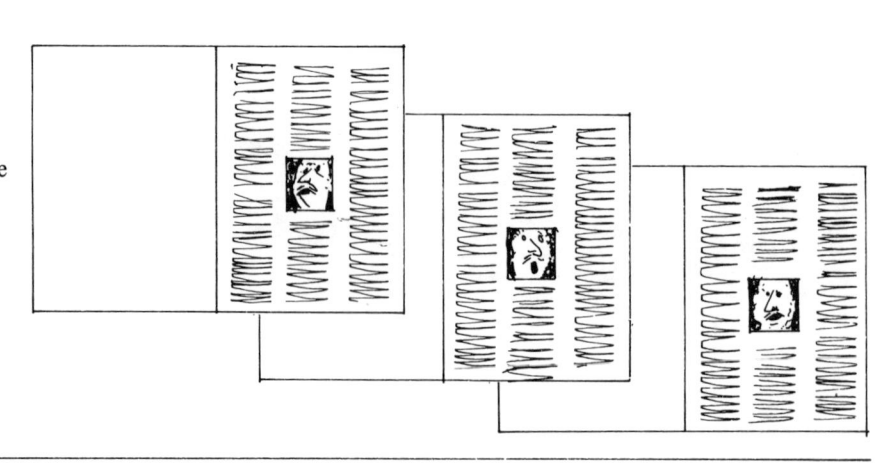

Clustering mugshots of various sizes: this is very decorative and fun to look at, but often a dangerous ploy to attempt, since many people misinterpret size as "importance." What a pity.

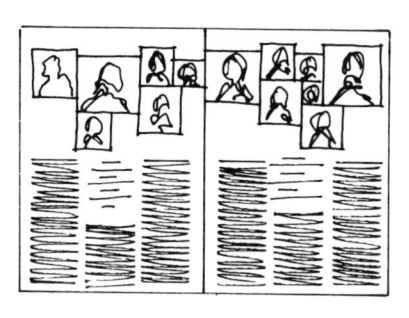

44

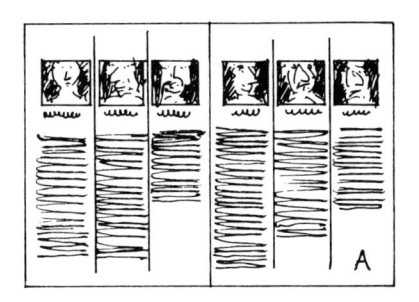

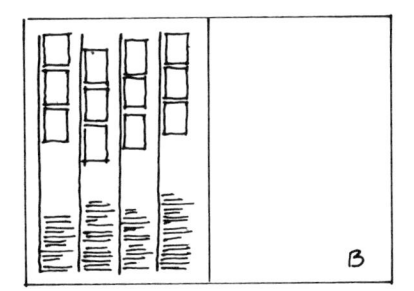

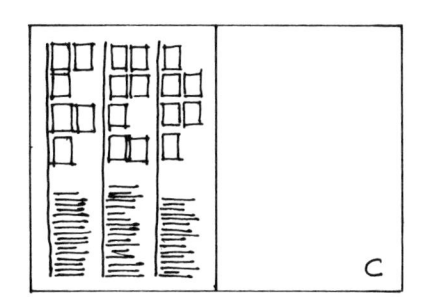

Placing mugshots next, or attached, to rules expands their effectiveness since it creates a double patterning (the mugs themselves, pictorial; and the rules, geometric).

In example A, the mugshots create a horizontal emphasis strong enough to camouflage the irregularity of the type beneath them.

In example B, equal-sized postage stamp mugshots appear more interesting because their placement is slightly staggered; the rules pull them together and make it possible to create this subtle variegation. Since the relationship between mugs within each group remains constant, it is easy to make such a trick.

In example C, arbitrarily omitted mugs within a rigid pattern framework make it more interesting to look at. Note that in both B and C the words have been pulled away from the mugshots, to allow the photos to be as decorative as possible, and the words at the foot of each column act as foils to the pictures above.

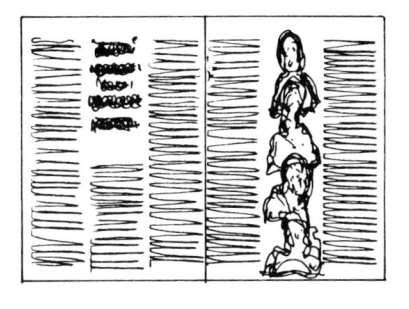

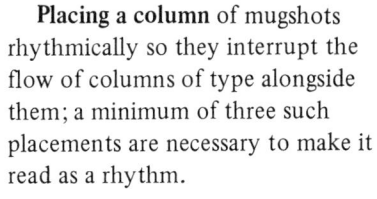

Placing a column of mugshots rhythmically so they interrupt the flow of columns of type alongside them; a minimum of three such placements are necessary to make it read as a rhythm.

Silhouetting and overlapping: here's where the most fun lies. Whether the frieze runs at the top or the bottom of the page also affects the handling of the text and the placement of the names.

If you can get away with overlapping mugshots of varied sizes in spite of the possible misinterpretation, you can create interesting scenes. It is also the cheapest possible way of combining a number of pictures, for you just have to cut out the originals (at whatever scale they came to you) and stick them together. And you skip the expensive nuisance step of re-shooting to get all originals to the same measurement between top of head and chin—which is the easiest way of getting them in scale with each other.

In such mugshot scenes, try to keep the eye level constant—it looks more natural that way.

45

If the pocket is right, it's wrong

This goes under the category of "Things we never knew to ask about," but there is, indeed, a way of making sure your pictures appear the right way 'round. It falls into two categories: the common sense (or obvious) category and the technical (or nobody ever told us about) category.

First, the *obvious:* if the lettering or street signs or billboards read backwards, then you know your picture is flopped. Exception: if it comes from somewhere where reading right-to-left is the proper way to do things. Problem: how do you know if the Arabic is flopped? Not unless you can read it. Solution: ask somebody who does.

Other good signs: if the chap's breast pocket is on HIS right side, then it's on the wrong side. Great help in deciding about mugshots, except when the subject is informally attired in T-shirt (or nothing).

Buttons help: men button clothes left-over-right. Women do it right-over-left. Come to think of it, one wonders why? But be that as it may, buttons are a good clue. You must put yourself in the place of the mugshot subject and imagine how he/she gets undressed. This is part of the fun of being an editor—never completely understood by the boss, who misinterprets such studying as daydreaming or goofing off!

Steering-wheels on cars are on the left (except in England) but the outside rear-view mirror is a more visible landmark. So, by the way, is the way the car is placed on the roadway. Exception: in case of a crash, in which case you're in trouble, too.

They say that south of the Equator the water runs down the bathtub drain anticlockwise, whereas up here the little whirlpool flows clockwise. That gets to be important as a clue if you are doing a movie.

Second, the *technical:*

In black-and-white prints, you can't tell except by the image itself. But if you have the negatives available for checking, you can then tell two ways: the dull side of the negative must face away from you (the shiny side must therefore be towards you). If you're seeing the picture that way, the image will read correctly. The other way is to look for the words printed on the film itself—various trademark words—that must be legible for you if you are looking at the film the right way. Contact prints that also show the edges of the film have the words printed visibly, too.

In color, the same principle holds true: the dull side must face away from you, the shiny side towards you. But here it is often quite difficult to decide which is dull and which is shiny—various films have various finishes on the emulsion side. 35mm slides are the easiest because on them, the emulsion side has ridges separating color edges; you can see them best by looking at the slide at a slight angle, letting the light bounce off it. If there are tiny ridges on it, then that must be the emulsion side, which ought to face away from you.

Alas, this doesn't work on large transparencies. Here you have to depend on the words on the film (which must not read backwards, if you are to be correct!) or on the *notches.* In sheet film—anything from a 4x5 up—the film actually has a set of notches cut out from a corner. These notches are there for a very practical reason: to tell the photo-lab technician which way to print the picture (something he must be able to determine in the dark!). They have a further wrinkle in that each type of film bears its own particular pattern of notches—much like Morse code in 3-d—to ensure correct processing. But the secret of all of this: the notches must appear in the top left-hand corner, on

(which way 'round is the picture?)

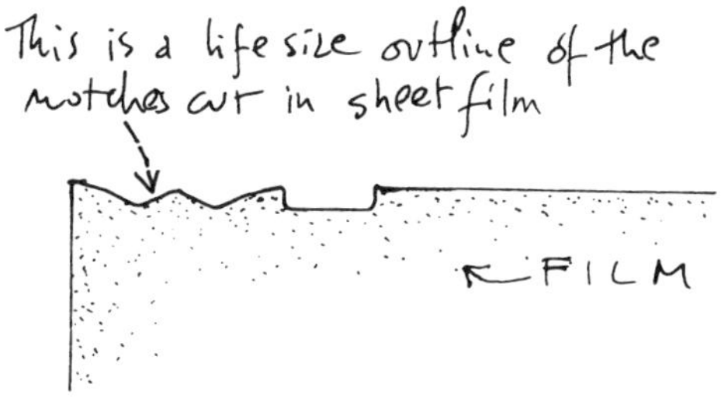

This is a life size outline of the notches cut in sheet film → [drawing] ← FILM

the top edge of the film *(see drawing)*. It makes no difference whether the photo is a "vertical" or a "horizontal," those notches must appear top-left-at-top, when you turn the film to determine the correct viewing side.

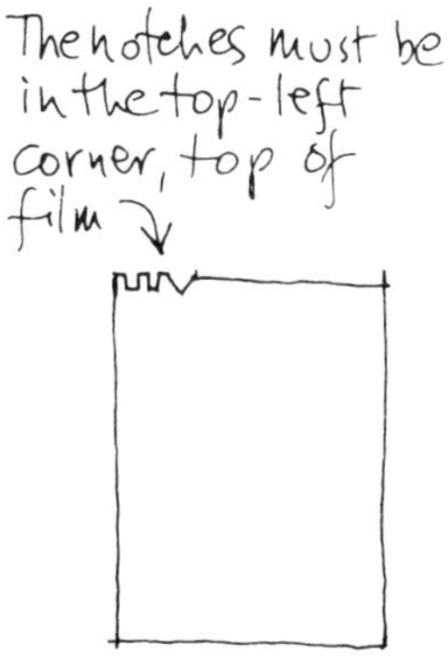

The notches must be in the top-left corner, top of film ↓

The photo can be vertical or horizontal — the notches must go top-left-top rows

Exception: if the transparency you have is a duplicate, you are in trouble, because duplicates are often made emulsion-side-to-emulsion-side in order to make the dupe with optimal quality. And, obviously, in that case the notches are on the wrong side. How can you tell? You can't, except if you can read the notches and determine that the material used is duplicating film. (Nobody but a technician can do *that!*) What to do? There is only one solution: guess. You have a 50-50 chance of being right, which is pretty good odds. But tip the scales in your favor by saying the secret words*, mark up the copy and send it to the printer.

Be sure to check for flopped photos when the "blues" come in from the printer. (Or "vandykes," "brownlines" or whatever the local nomenclature is for what used to be called "page proofs.") It is very easy for the printer to make a mistake in stripping by turning over a piece of negative film and thus forcing the chap's pocket to be on the right, which is wrong.

*"To hell with it!"

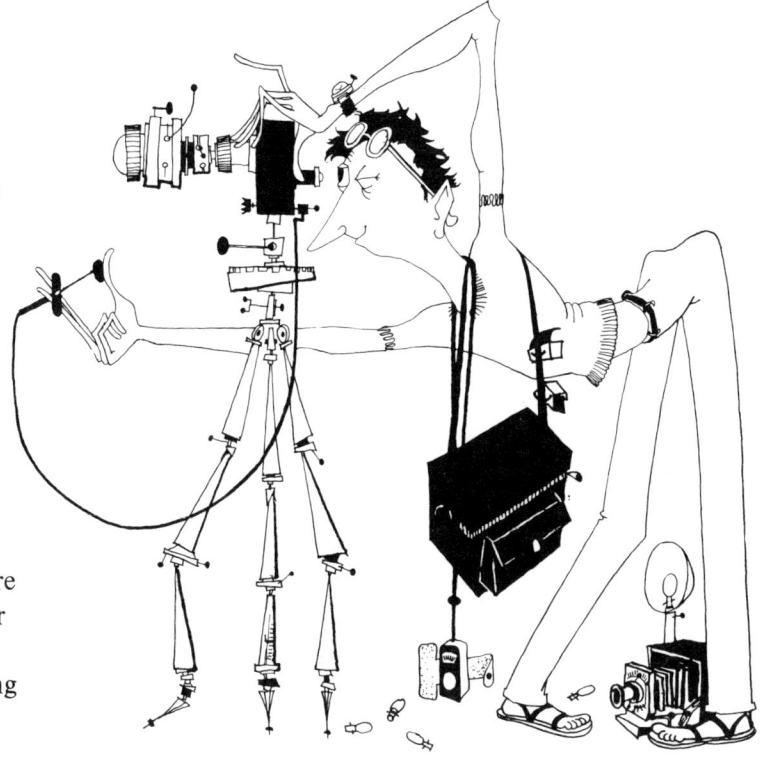

Left-to-right and the sticky edge

It is useful to remember that type (written on the typewriter or set in type on any other sort of machinery) sets a visual flow—it has a left-to-right direction. We read from left to right, we also automatically organize the logical sequencing or flow of material from left to right, and we were taught at school that diagrams start at zero at the bottom left-hand corner and flow up or down from there.

This capacity can be made use of to make words into pictures, like this, for instance:

WHY DO OTHER PEOPLES' STOCKS GO UP WHEN MINE ONLY GO DOWN?

This diagrammatization (sorry about such a word) depends on our instinctive understanding of the left-to-right charting to make the trick work. OK, this may not be too useful too often. But when it makes good editorial sense, use it: the payoff in liveliness and the kudos for inventiveness you'll garner will balance the sleepless night you'll spend wondering whether you aren't making a dreadful mistake.

It feels normal to start reading at left; we are used to reading lines that start at a justified left-hand edge. The eye knows where to return to read the next line. If the right-hand margin is set ragged or unjustified, we don't mind: more and more text is being set rag-right because the typesetting is actually improved. The spacing of characters can retain its normal, standard, correct proportion instead of having to be widened in order to open up to justify to a specific measure. But be that as it may, rag-right setting presents no problems for the reader's eye to follow from line to line.

However, if we reverse the procedure and set a rigid, justified right-hand margin, and set the text ragged on the left, much confusion ensues: the eye has to search for the start of the succeeding line of type and such a task becomes a decided nuisance. It therefore reduces ease of reading

```
This is a line of type
and this is a second one
followed by
a third one, all
of varied length, set
flush left.
Easy to read.
```

```
         This is a line of type
     and this is a second one
                   followed by
               a third one,all
         of varied length, set
                  flush right.
                 Hard to read.
```

considerably. However, we can do it for a few lines under special circumstances when it makes sense to do so—in situations of display type in heads or decks, or in short captions or cutlines.

A separate capacity brought about by the justified edge in contrast to the ragged edge is that of a straight edge appearing to "stick to" whatever is near it. If a block of type with short lines is set flush *right* and ragged on the left, then it appears weighted towards the right. Its center of gravity is

```
    This paragraph
       has a center
         of gravity
         pulling it
               over
             to the
         right -- its
           vertical
               edge
```

pulled over to the right, and it seems to belong to whatever is at right. Taking it the other way around: if the same is set flush left and ragged right, it is less startling than the other example

```
This paragraph
has a center
of gravity
pulling it
over
to the
left -- its
vertical
edge
```

because we are used to seeing this format more often—but the same weight-distribution and stickiness works towards the left this time.

It follows, therefore, that in logical page makeup, the proper placement for the caption relative to the picture is to get the vertically justified edge of the caption next to the appropriate vertical side of the picture, so the two can glue together naturally:

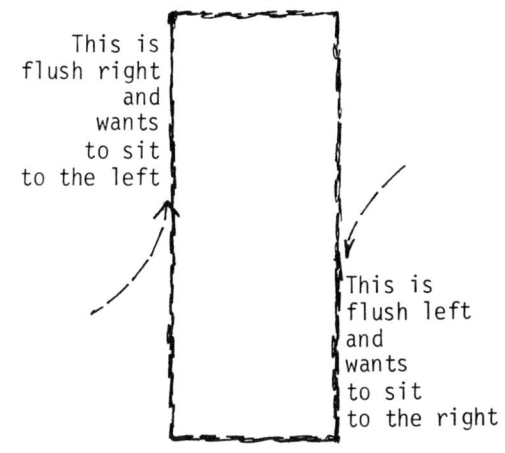

```
     This is
 flush right
         and
       wants
      to sit
  to the left
```

```
This is
flush left
and
wants
to sit
to the right
```

This same stickiness works vertically, in placing the caption above or below the picture. Perhaps this isn't quite as obvious, but it is definitely an important element that can impart crispness and stylishness to a publication. Clean alignment of verticals feels right: it bespeaks care in assembly—professional finish.

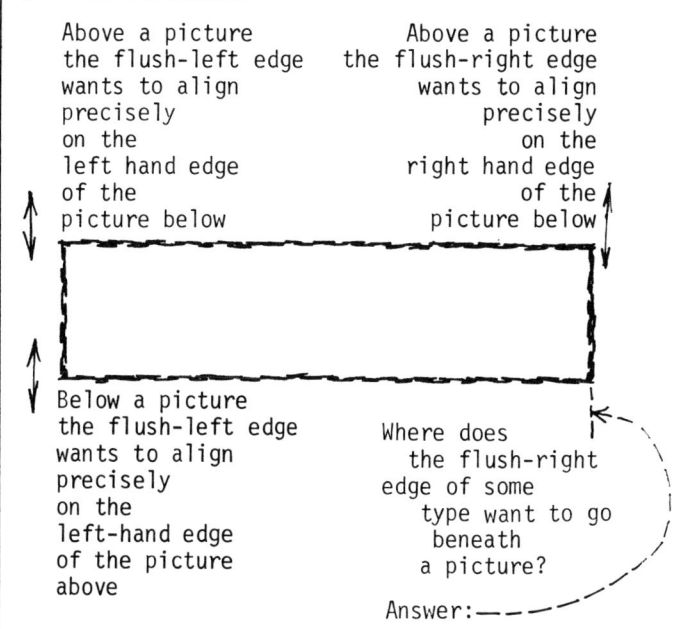

```
Above a picture
the flush-left edge
wants to align
precisely
on the
left hand edge
of the
picture below
```

```
Above a picture
the flush-right edge
wants to align
precisely
on the
right hand edge
of the
picture below
```

```
Below a picture
the flush-left edge
wants to align
precisely
on the
left-hand edge
of the picture
above
```

```
Where does
   the flush-right
   edge of some
      type want to go
      beneath
      a picture?
   Answer:
```

Now if you take this principle to its logical conclusion (as I believe you should), you'll also be aware of the handsomeness and logic derived from aligning the type with the top or bottom of the picture. That way you are using BOTH sticky edges of the caption: the vertically aligned one as well as the horizontal one at top or bottom (whichever you are using). It sounds ridiculously complicated but is equally ridiculously simple.

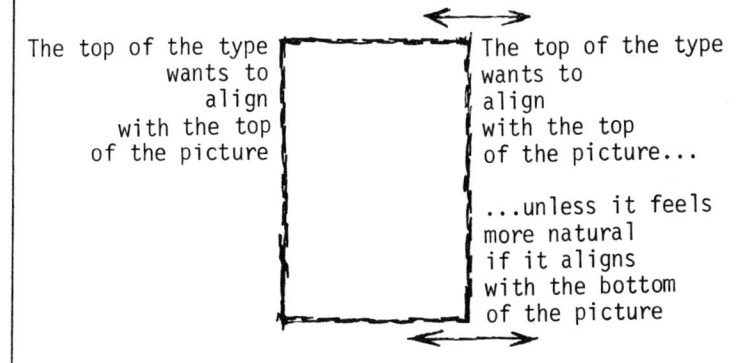

```
The top of the type
        wants to
          align
     with the top
      of the picture
```

```
The top of the type
wants to
align
with the top
of the picture...

...unless it feels
more natural
if it aligns
with the bottom
of the picture
```

So, you ask, when does it make sense to center a caption on a picture? Off the top of my head I would say "never"—mostly because it also happens to divide whatever nice hunk of white space you may have left over into two unimpressive pieces.

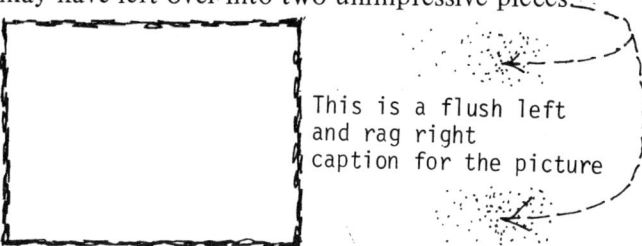

```
This is a flush left
and rag right
caption for the picture
```

But it is folly ever to say "never" to an editor.

49

Getting an artist to draw the drawing you want

There should be more editorial involvement in this than there usually is. Most editors leave it up to the artist's intuition (taste? preference? predilection? habit?) to render the subject in the way they see fit, little realizing that the style of draftsmanship affects the character of what is being depicted.

The subtle differences in the ways the lines are drawn as well as the materials used, create various moods of expression that can influence the viewer into totally different interpretations, and thus affect the meaning of the editorial message. Art also prejudices readers *before* they have read the story, for readers look at the pictures before they tackle the words.

Furthermore, the style of the art affects the character of the printed piece as a whole by its cumulative impression of playfulness or seriousness, sketchiness or precision, looseness or technicality and so on. Enough reasons why editors ought to become more knowledgeable, involved and confident in their own judgment?

DRAWINGS BY VICTORIA F. SKOMAL

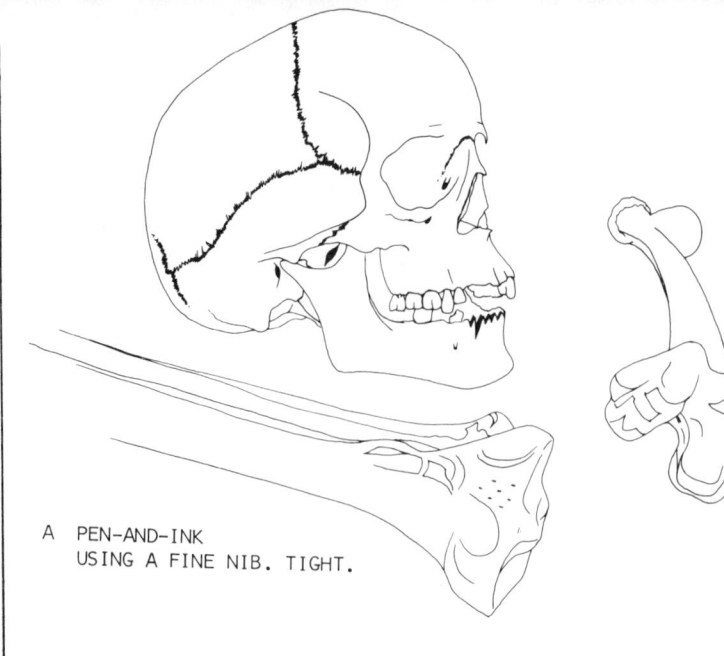

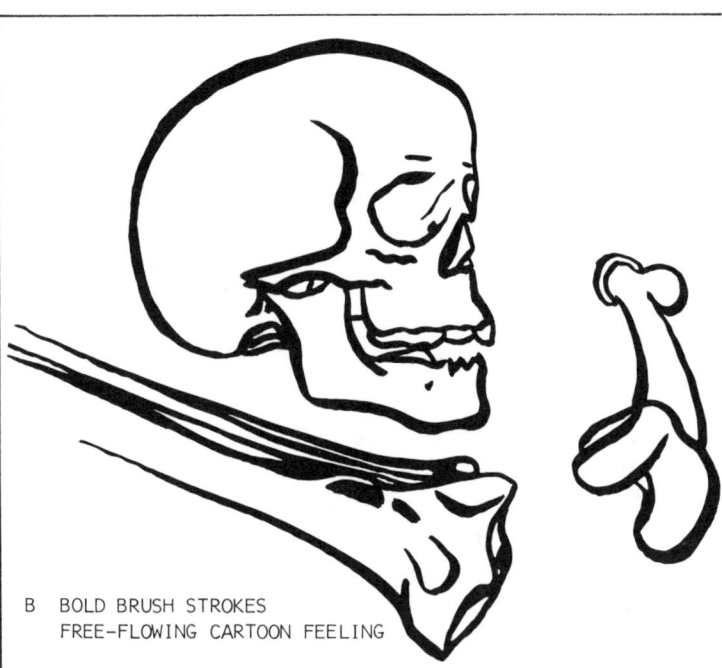

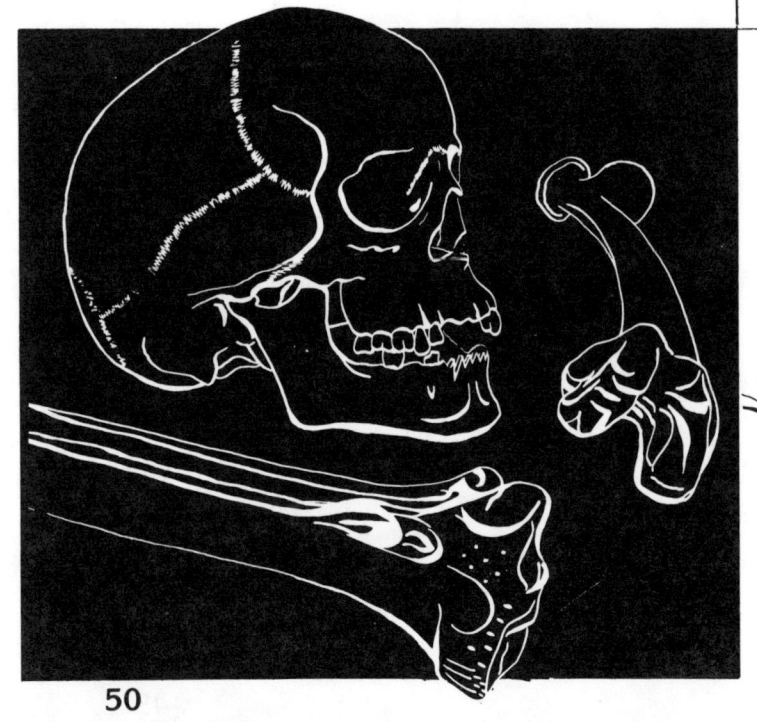

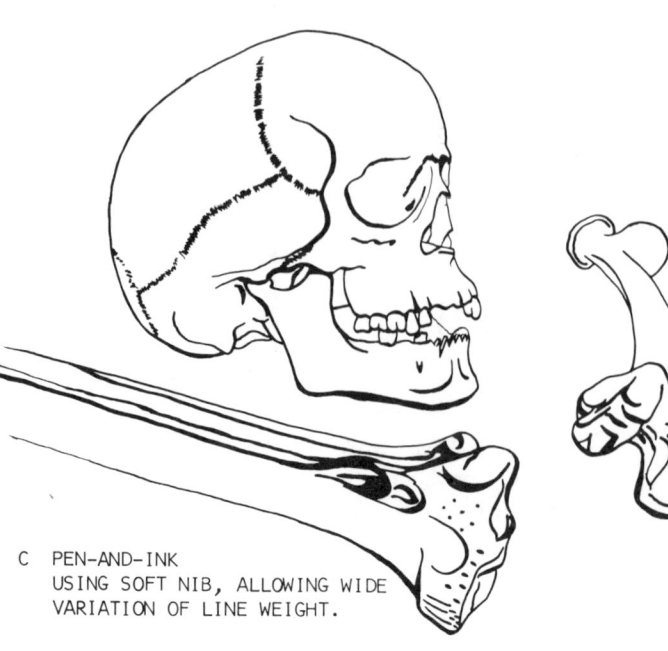

A PEN-AND-INK
USING A FINE NIB. TIGHT.

B BOLD BRUSH STROKES
FREE-FLOWING CARTOON FEELING

C PEN-AND-INK
USING SOFT NIB, ALLOWING WIDE VARIATION OF LINE WEIGHT.

50

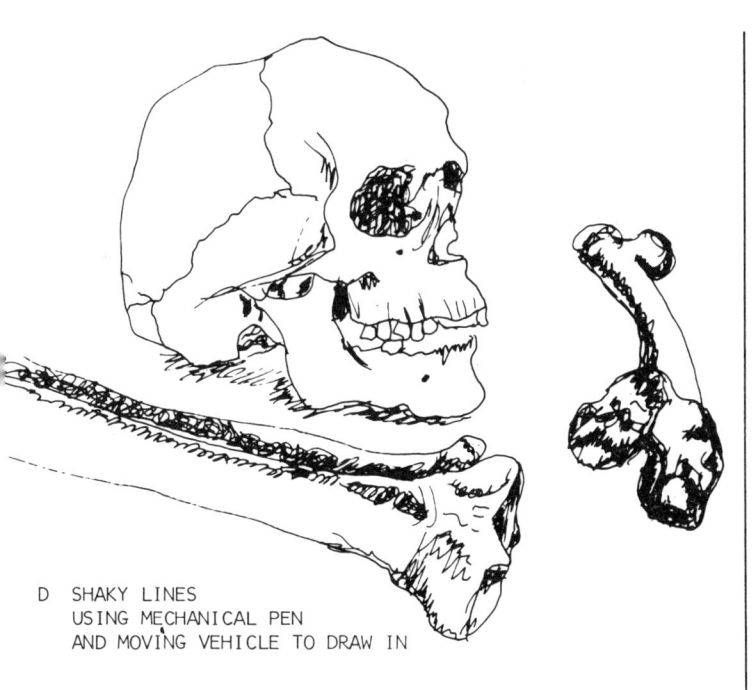

D SHAKY LINES
   USING MECHANICAL PEN
   AND MOVING VEHICLE TO DRAW IN

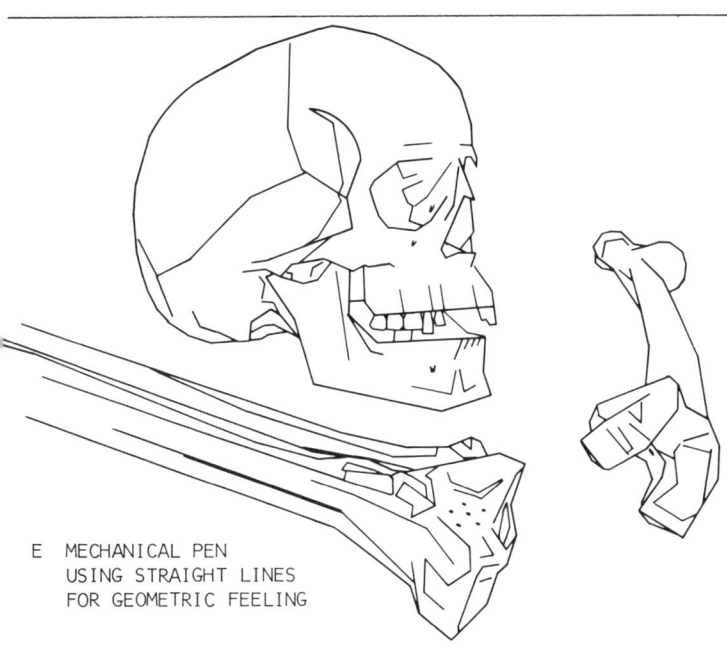

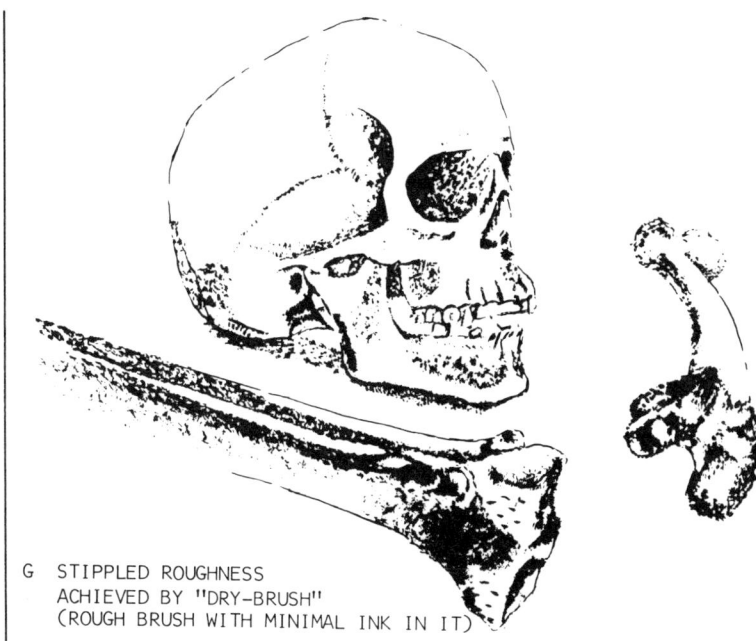

G STIPPLED ROUGHNESS
   ACHIEVED BY "DRY-BRUSH"
   (ROUGH BRUSH WITH MINIMAL INK IN IT)

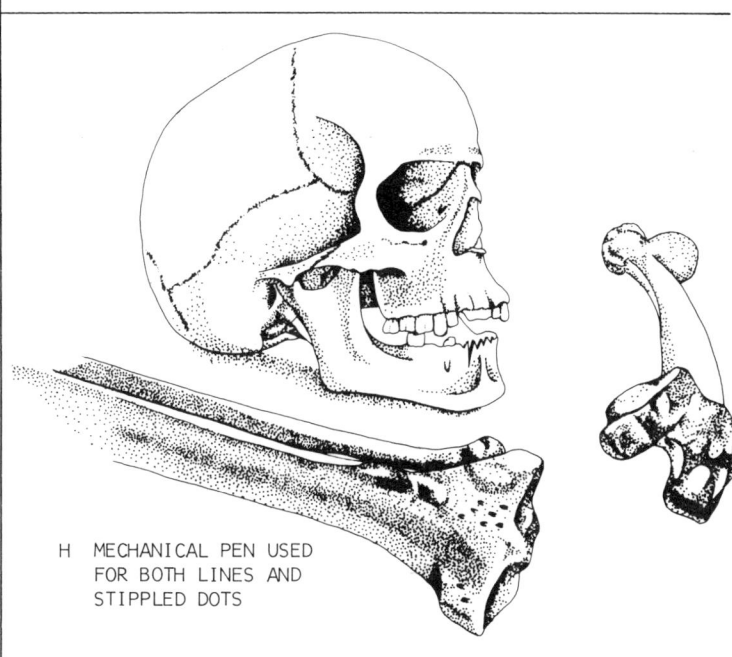

E MECHANICAL PEN
   USING STRAIGHT LINES
   FOR GEOMETRIC FEELING

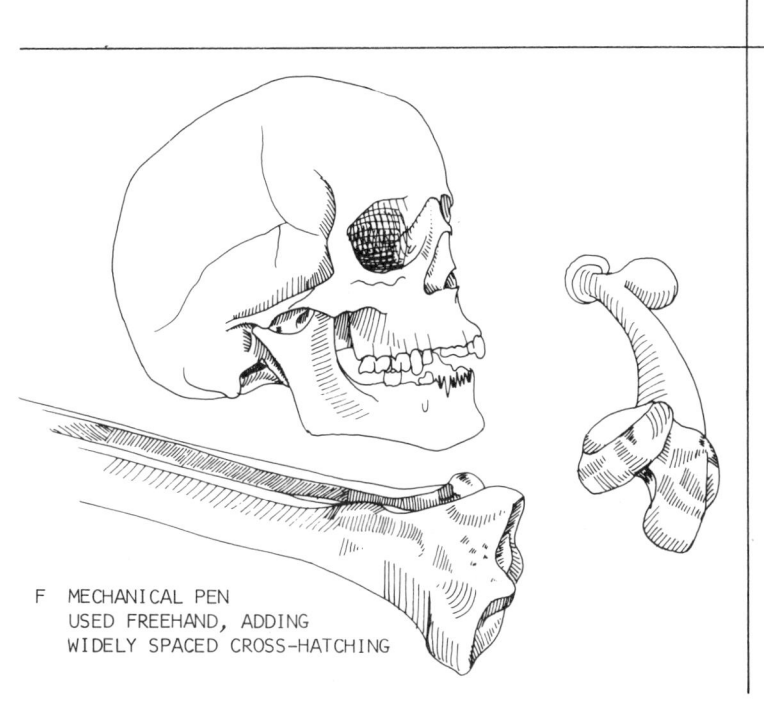

H MECHANICAL PEN USED
   FOR BOTH LINES AND
   STIPPLED DOTS

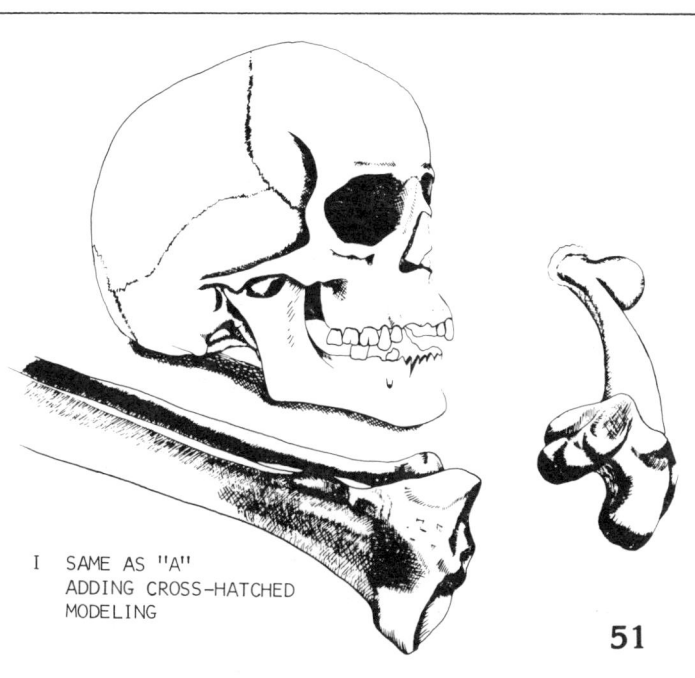

F MECHANICAL PEN
   USED FREEHAND, ADDING
   WIDELY SPACED CROSS-HATCHING

I SAME AS "A"
   ADDING CROSS-HATCHED
   MODELING

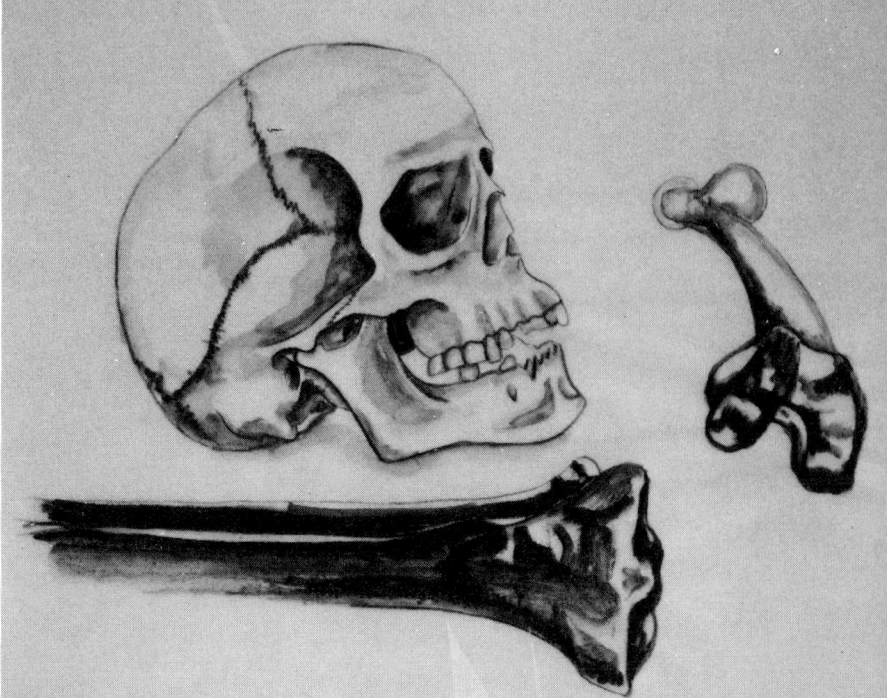

These drawings were made by medical illustrator Victoria Skomal of Fairfield, CT. She sat next to my mother on a train from New York and (mothers being what they are) came to show me her portfolio the next day. I saw the versatility of her draftsmanship and suggested she draw up as many variations on a skull theme as she could (before going out of her own!).

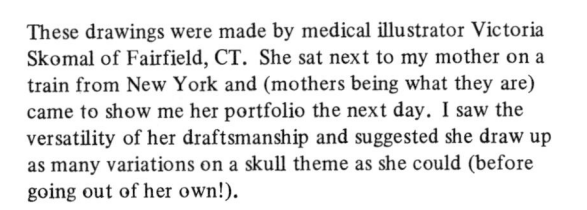

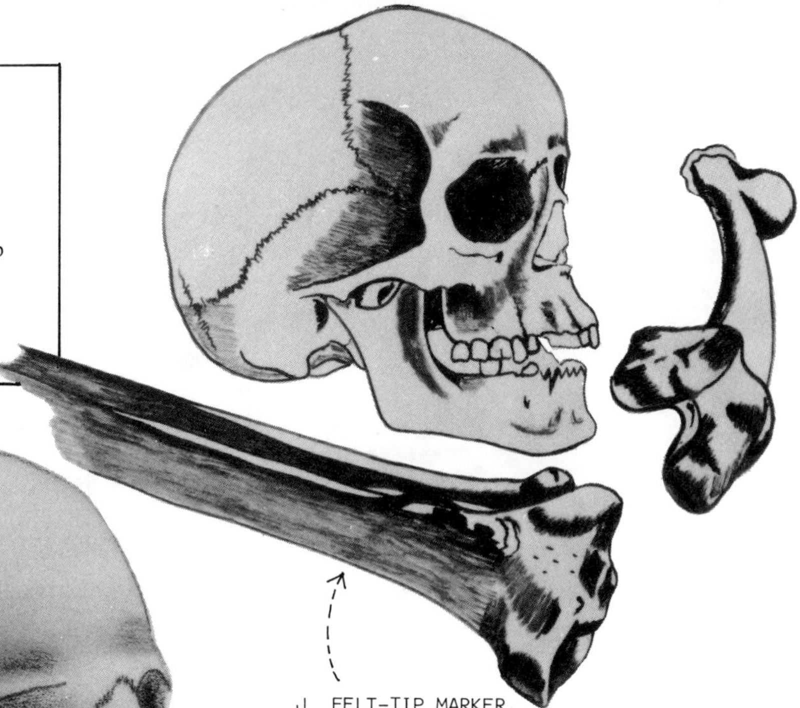

J FELT-TIP MARKER.
TO RETAIN VARIATION OF "COLOR" IN THE LINES, A HALFTONE MUST BE MADE, SAME AS EXAMPLE "L" BELOW. TO GET RID OF THE BACKGROUND, EITHER THE PRINTER SILHOUETTES THE PARTS INTENDED TO PRINT, OR THEY ARE CUT OUT WITH SCISSORS FROM A "VELOX" (A PAPER PRINT OF THE HALFTONE) AND PASTED ON THE MECHANICAL, AS WAS DONE HERE.

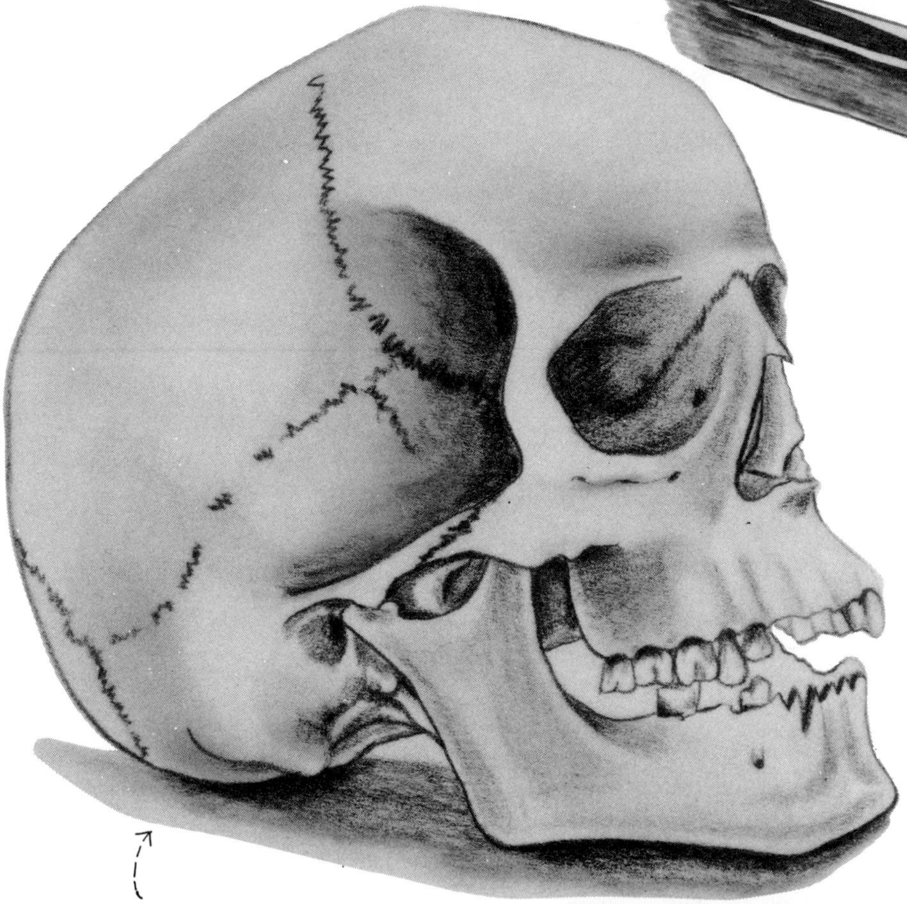

L WATERCOLOR RENDERING REPRODUCED AS A STRAIGHT HALFTONE

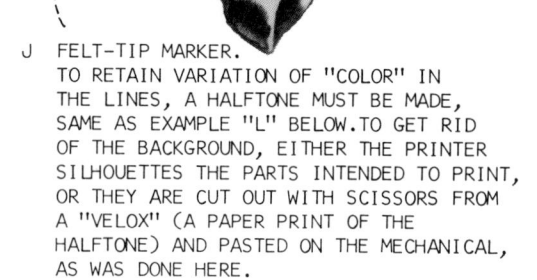

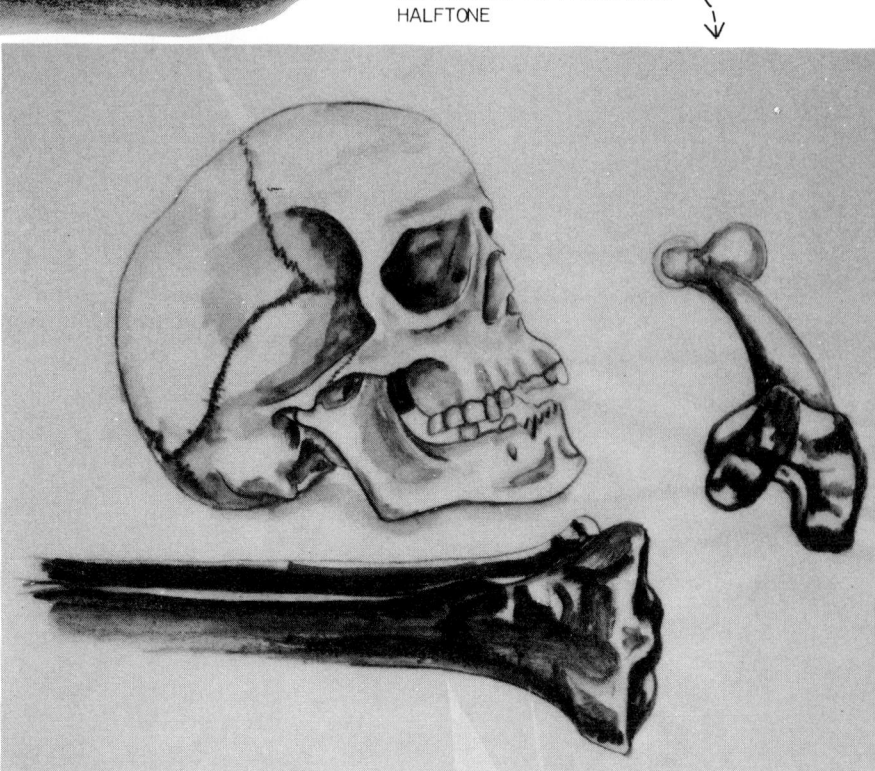

K PENCIL RENDERING
USING A SOFT, BLACK CRAYON. REPRODUCED HERE AT ORIGINAL SIZE TO SHOW SUBTLETY OF TONAL VALUES. THE GREATER THE REDUCTION, THE MORE LOSS OF TONALITIES RESULTS.

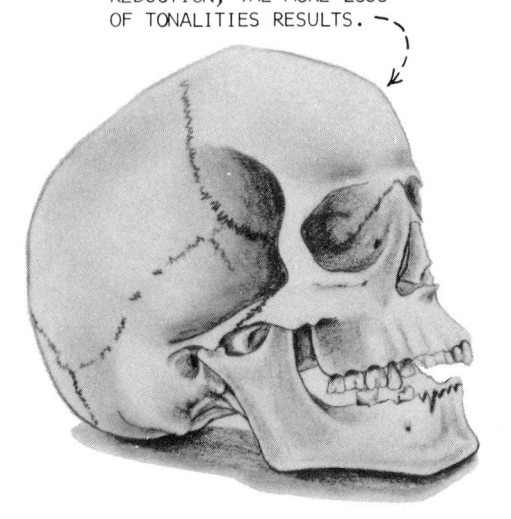

52

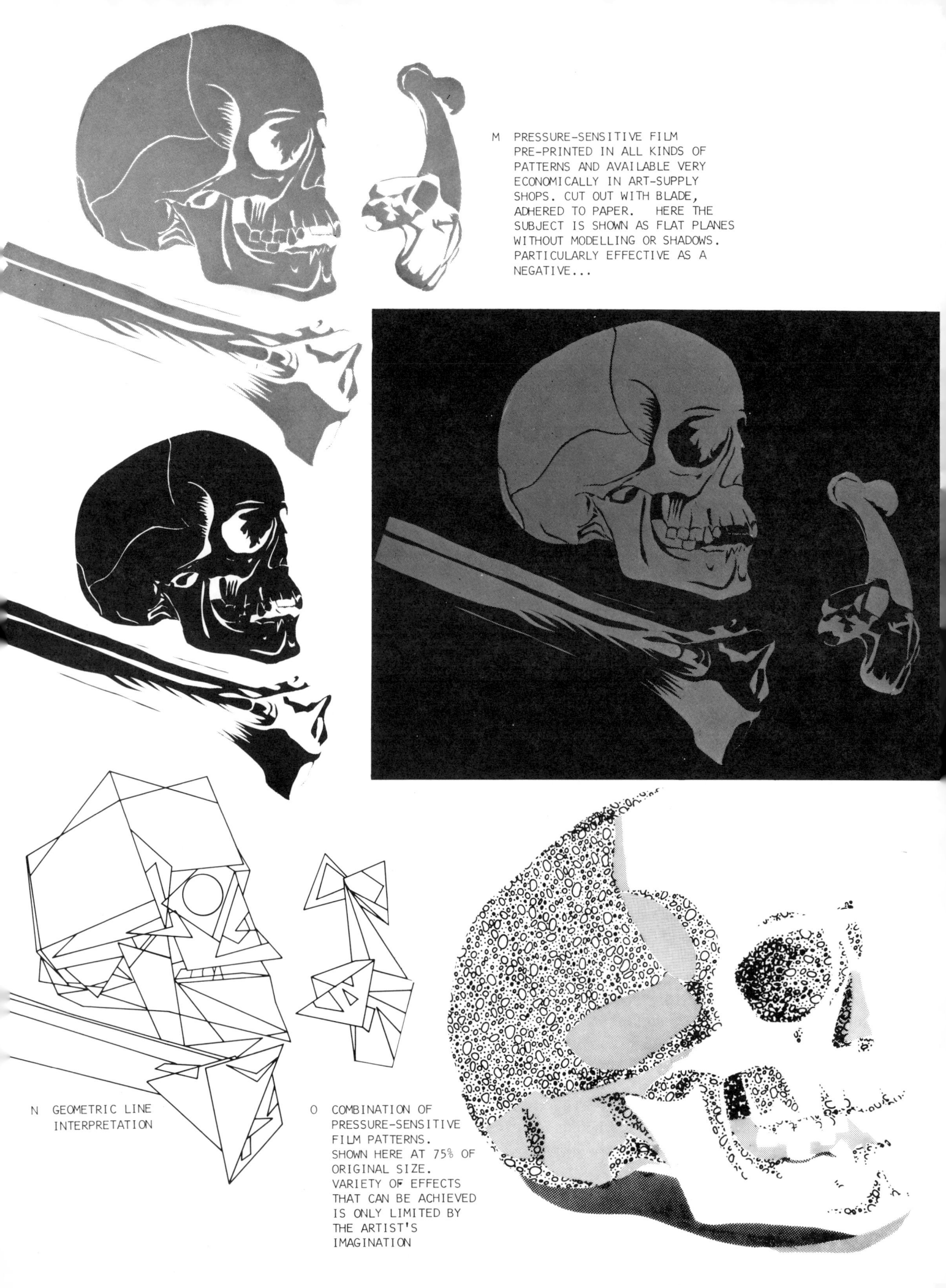

M PRESSURE-SENSITIVE FILM PRE-PRINTED IN ALL KINDS OF PATTERNS AND AVAILABLE VERY ECONOMICALLY IN ART-SUPPLY SHOPS. CUT OUT WITH BLADE, ADHERED TO PAPER. HERE THE SUBJECT IS SHOWN AS FLAT PLANES WITHOUT MODELLING OR SHADOWS. PARTICULARLY EFFECTIVE AS A NEGATIVE...

N GEOMETRIC LINE INTERPRETATION

O COMBINATION OF PRESSURE-SENSITIVE FILM PATTERNS. SHOWN HERE AT 75% OF ORIGINAL SIZE. VARIETY OF EFFECTS THAT CAN BE ACHIEVED IS ONLY LIMITED BY THE ARTIST'S IMAGINATION

For goodness' sake get on with it!

Us editors* are nothing if not human. That's why we all tend to put off what we don't enjoy or dread doing until the last possible moment. That's why layout gets postponed until it becomes inescapable, and at that critical point we then trade thought for expediency. We throw the thing together the best way it happens to fit. That's all we can do under the crazy circumstances we made for ourselves.

We don't expect too much of those layouts, given the wonderful excuse of "not enough time." We just cannot step back to examine what we've been doing before it is committed to the printer for duplication by the thousands —nor do we really want to, because we're a bit afraid of that very examination. We'd just as soon avoid noticing those oh-the-heck-with-it compromises we forced ourselves into making through our own mismanagement of time.

Instead, we fall back on rationalizations, on those conventional wisdoms, those tried-and-true maxims remembered from some distant high-school art adviser (or, worse, English teacher doubling as journalism instructor) or workshop leader or even consultant. And they —the wisdoms—are probably taken out of context and were probably never understood thoroughly in the first place. Yet we build our product on a foundation of trite generalizations which tell us nonsense like "never trap the thingumajig" or "never jump the whatsis" or "whenever you do the flumadiddle, you must follow it with a doohick"! All generalizations are false (including this one). No, that way of working is obviously wrong.

It is just as silly to telescope the job of page-arranging, which is the final step of the *editing* process, into minimal time at the end. That used to be S.O.P. on the high school yearbook and may even have been the way that the college magazine you worked on was put together. It is also the normal way for newspapers to operate.

BUT: Our professionally made periodicals cannot be handled the same way our childish experiments were. Nor must we think of them as slow newspapers, in spite of their possible similarity of shape, size and material.

The essential difference between periodicals and newspapers is one of *quality;* and that quality is made evident by thinking the articles through in the time available for their creation. Thus the excuse for loose, inexpressive, even shoddy, make-up is valid for a newspaper; it implies such fast closing, such concentration on the hard-news-value of the content, that a degree of imprecision (thrown-togetherness) may even help the image.

Besides, on a newspaper we just have to go by the accepted, standard methods and rules. We'd be foolish not to use them as shortcuts to getting the issue to bed. Furthermore, the reader expects the product to be put together a certain way.

A periodical, though, has much less time pressure to contend with. That doesn't mean that the short-handed editor isn't always in a rush! There isn't an editor in the Western world who complains of too much time. There isn't a publication that isn't under-staffed. But this is *our* secret. How we solve it is nobody's business but our own—so long as we solve it. It ought never be allowed to affect the excellence of our product.

How? That depends on individual circumstances. And that is a neat way to gloss over THAT part of the argument. Let's return to the philosophy.

Why ought we avoid using those catch-phrase nostrums and precepts for our products? Because they bottle up our potential for originality. They stop us from thinking creatively. How does one think creatively in this area? By taking the editing process two steps beyond the manuscript stage— steps that are as important to the final result as the writing itself and, therefore, an integral part of the editor's task.

---

*Yes, I know it should be "We editors" but that's inhuman precision!

Step 1: Figure out the emphasis.
Step 2: Make that emphasis visible on the page.

The first step is a mental/verbal process. The second, a mental/visual process.

Once you know what the significance of the story is *(to your reader!),* you can decide on which elements to put your emphasis: be they pictorial, verbal, graphic, or a meld of them all.

Emphasis—in whatever form it may take—is the very soul of the art of publishing. Just running a story straight may well be good enough for a newspaper, but it is definitely not good enough for a periodical. The essence of a newspaper is in its up-to-dateness. The essence of a periodical is that it interprets the news into information of use to its readers. It is therefore a much more intimate, personalized product. *It must therefore be much more carefully assembled.*

This is where "design" comes in. I put the word design in quotes on purpose. I could have said *so-called design,* thus perhaps denigrating it too much. But my purpose is not to knock "art," "layout," "page makeup"—by any means. I love it and honor it. And it is precisely because I do that I want to debunk it of its misunderstood arcane esoterica.

Design is NOT a bunch of secrets only revealed to some wild-eyed practitioners. It is, instead, a working tool for the working editor. When design is done for its own sake, then it is indeed a scary monster (depending, as it does, on subjective "liking"—something nobody can argue about). But when you see design as just a means of calling the readers' attention to that which you, as editor, consider the important element, then design is no longer art for art's sake. It becomes a technique for communication's sake.

That's when it becomes obvious that anybody with a modicum of editorial insight and decisiveness can master it. There are no rules. Honestly. Just common sense and logic. If what you feel like doing makes sense for the story, and makes sense in the context within which the story will be seen, then you ought to do it—whatever the "it" may be. Forget the reasons why not. Forget those prosaic promises, those platitudinous analects. Follow what is your most important asset: your journalistic instinct.

Think the problem through, then lay it out so the reader cannot help but notice whatever you deem to be the crucial element in the story. Make it big. . .run it in color. . .at an angle. . .upside down. . .in green with pink spots. It doesn't matter how you do it or what you do, so long as the journalism is right. That's what will guarantee appropriate excitement and liveliness. Anyway, once you've got your Big Point down, you arrange the supporting material around it. . . .

But you cannot do this sort of in-depth thinking when you have 18 pages to lay out between now and 10 tonight, when the printer's last pickup comes around. If that's all the time you have, no wonder you cannot produce anything better than the usually bland pap.

Instead, start laying out as soon as the galleys for each story arrive. Inspiration won't come next week at deadline time. On the contrary, by then you'll have forgotten the important things worthy of emphasis in the story that right now is at the forefront of your mind. If you pin the layout down right now, as an integral step in your editorial thinking, then each story will have a shape which is an organic development of its inner editorial meaning. That is what is going to make it interesting. Not superficially cosmetically pretty.

So: Conquer that mistrust of makeup! (Isn't it significant that we use "cosmetic" as a pejorative term when discussing "page makeup"?) See it for what it is—and DO get on with it!

NC 1000 .W448 1981 c.1